"Dr. Cooper captures in exquisite and clean prose the essence and the complexity of Liberia culture. He writes of his own experiences growing up in Liberia; his fascinating and circuitous journey to the United States and his encounters with a culture alien to his own, but which he is able to adopt with enviable alacrity. The novel is written in his unique style of humor and candor, leaving the reader at times chuckling or laughing out loud. The book is a page-turner.

"We discover John Bower's insatiable and iconic quest for knowledge as he pursues his fascinating career before returning to his native Liberia, where he pursues is life long goal of helping his people and delivering the best health care anywhere along the West African coast.

"Liberia became a better country with the return of this Guinea Fowl. A compelling and refreshing read."

Joseph Diggs, M.D.
Vanderbilt University School of Medicine, Nashville, Tennessee

"This book is an inspiration to all who will read it. Because of the wealth of information, it is a "must read" for anyone who would like to learn about the history and culture of Liberia, this unique country located on the west coast of Africa. The portrayal and presentation of the subject matter are phenomenal.

"Being the clinician Dr. Cooper was, medical students as well as doctors should find this book a learning experience as they read some of the episodes Dr. Cooper expertly relates through the character of Dr. John Bowers.

"Dr. Cooper has left a superb legacy by any standard."

Alma van Ransalier Parker, Spouse of Colonel C. Donald Parker, U.S. Foreign Service Officer in Liberia, 1968 – 1970.

The Return of the Guinea Fowl:

An Autobiographical Novel of a Liberian Doctor

By Henry Nehemiah Cooper, M.D.

with Izetta Roberts Cooper,
Dawn Cooper Barnes, Ph.D. and Kyra E. Hicks

ISBN-13: 978-1460949351   ISBN-10: 1460949358

The guinea fowl on the cover was photographed at Kirstenbosch National Botanical Garden, Cape Town, South Africa, September 2009 by Lisa Cooper Green, MD, MPH.

Cover Design: ManjariGraphics

Dedication

To his parents,

Charles Henry Cooper and MaryAnn Dabadolo Cooper (nee Johnson)

And all of the patients of Henry Nehemiah Cooper, M.D.

I shall pass through
This world but once.
Any good therefore
That I can do or any
Kindness that I can
Show to any human
Being, let me do it now.
Let me not defer or
Neglect it for I shall
Not pass this way
again.

William Penn

"There are many people who helped me along the way; I only feel it's
fair that I help others along their way if I can."

Henry N. Cooper, M.D.

The Return of the Guinea Fowl:
An Autobiographical Novel of a Liberian Doctor
Contents

Acknowledgements

This book has been more than twenty-five years in the making. So many dear friends have been supportive. Specifically, we want to thank:

Dr. Matthew Walker (1906 – 1978), who is internationally recognized as a pioneer in medicine and surgery and an educator of doctors and surgeons. We are grateful for the influence of Dr. Walker, teacher and mentor of Dr. Henry N. Cooper at Meharry Medical College. Dr. Cooper greatly admired Dr. Walker and called him "Chief."

Dr. Charles Whitten (1922 – 2008), physician, professor and specialist in sickle cell disease was Dr. Cooper's dear friend and colleague. Dr. Whitten's letter inviting Dr. Cooper to attend a health conference in the U.S. was helpful in enabling Dr. Cooper to leave Liberia soon after that country's bloody *coup d'etat* in 1980.

Dr. Adell Patton, Jr., a successful medical researcher and historian, was helpful in research and compiling an extensive bibliography by and about Dr. Cooper.

Dr. Lisa A. Cooper Green, daughter of Dr. Henry N. Cooper, a physician and professor at Johns Hopkins University School of Medicine and MacArthur Fellow, was helpful in editing medical portions of this book and providing many of the pictures.

Ambassador Julius W. Walker, Jr. (1927 – 2003) and his wife, **Savannah**, career diplomats of the United States of America Department of State, are dear friends who will always have a special place in our family's heart.

Henry N. Conway, Jr. and his late wife, **Ann**, are our very dear friends. We have such pleasant memories of life in Liberia with them and of a wonderful relationship.

Joseph and **Anna Richards**, special childhood friends of Dr. and Mrs. Cooper. We share many fond memories.

To "Miah" With Love – A Letter to My Husband

My darling Miah,

It is now over twenty-six years since you left me to be in eternity with our Lord. How I miss you! There is not a single day that I do not think of you. We were happily married for thirty-one years embracing as a foundation: love, support and respect. When I pray, I thank God for our life together. What beautiful years we shared with love, peace and prosperity. You were my best friend, my confidante, my love. We danced, we laughed, we cried, we shared and, in our little way, tried to make a difference in God's world. I am forever grateful to God.

We were blessed with three lovely children, grandchildren, relatives and friends. Although you did not see all the grands, they know their "Pappy," the name you gave them to call you. They call me "Mama." Little Devin left to be with you as so many dear ones – all of you are now in your new spiritual home with our Father and His Son. You would be so proud of our children. They are all making wonderful contributions in their respective professional fields.

I have a difficult time making it without you, and, at times, I feel so lonely and sad. There are so many things I would like to share with you. How I long for your thoughtful advice and strong arms; but then I remember what you said to me as you lay dying: "You are a strong woman, Lady." You kept saying that. Now I know why. You wanted me to be strong because you knew you had to leave me.

You dropped your head on my shoulder and said, "Where is Lady?"

"Here I am holding you."

"Lady," you said. This was your last word. Then you breathed your last breath. You were gone!

Oh, my God, so many things ran across my mind. How will I tell the children? How will I make it without you? How can I return to the U.S. without you?

I thought about the children's education, the grandchildren, the Cooper Clinic, living alone without you, managing in general. I can't even remember what all crowded my mind. Suddenly, I felt a calm. I felt consoled that I would soon join you and then we would be together again. This was a comforting thought. I have, however, made it for over twenty-six years. I have been strong at times and weak at times; however, I always think of your words, "You are a strong woman, Lady." And, I always pray.

There were the preparations for the funeral. Gracious Lord, what a funeral! Your people said goodbye to you in such an honorable way. So many friends and dignitaries, your patients, your colleagues, both professional and social, your community, your government, the Cooper Clinic family and your own family all came out to honor and express appreciation for you and your life's work – your wonderful contributions to humanity. I was overwhelmed.

You did not get to finish your novel. For years, I really wanted to pick up where you left off when your earthly life was ended. I tried so hard so many times only to get cold feet. I guess I didn't have closure and just couldn't cope. Guess what? I wrote a book, *Liberia - A Visit Through Books: A Selected Annotative Bibliography & Reflections of a Liberian Librarian.* You know I always loved books. Aren't you proud of me? I know you are and I can imagine you just smiling and giving me a big hug. You were always so loving and supportive.

The fact that I wrote a book has really given me the confidence that I can finish your book. Another factor, that has given me courage, is my recent trip home to Liberia where I visited your grave in Kormah, the village and burial place of you and your ancestors. As I sat on your grave, I made the decision to finish your book, *The Return of the Guinea Fowl.*

Our children Armah (Butch), Dawn and Lisa would like this also. In fact, Dawn had already done a lot by typing your handwritten pages into a manuscript and editing your work. Kyra Hicks, a friend and author who encouraged me to write and published my book, is also instrumental in this project. Finally, your cousin Armah Robert Johnson, who is very fond of you, has encouraged me to complete this work.

I have lived in Columbia, Maryland, U.S.A. since 1987. I have remained active in the church and social organizations and I enjoy volunteering with various groups. My greatest joy has been my role in helping to raise our grandchildren.

I hope you will be pleased with the way we completed your book. I have done my best; thinking all the while, how you would like it done.

Thank you for trusting me with your story.

I love you with all my heart and will forever. Until we meet again.

Your dear wife,

Lady

Izetta Roberts Cooper and H. Nehemiah Cooper, M.D., 1982

Introduction

If I should die and leave you here awhile,
Be not like others, sore undone, who keep
Long vigils by the silent dust, and weep.
For my sake turn again to life, and smile,
Nerving thy heart and trembling hand to do
Something to comfort weaker hearts than thine;
Complete these dear unfinished tasks of mine,
And I, perchance, may therein comfort you.

- Consolation

It never crossed my mind that it would be my lot to complete this book. It all started many years ago when "Miah" (short for Nehemiah, the name his family and friends called him) came home from work at the Cooper Clinic, his clinic, calling out to me: "I have a brainstorm, Mommy," as he affectionately called me at times. "I am going to write an autobiographical novel."

Starting in about 1978, he began to write his book; however, his busy work schedule and lifestyle in Liberia made it almost impossible. After the 1980 coup d'état in Liberia, when the Government of President William Tolbert was toppled, Miah was able to write again.

We had relocated to the United States; first to Howard University in Washington, D.C. , then to Nashville, Tennessee where he was on staff at Meharry Medical College as Professor of Surgery and Clinical Director of the International Center for Health Services. It was then that he had more time to concentrate on writing his book. Each evening as I sat and listened to the CBS Evening News with Dan Rather, Miah would sit with me and write notes for his book.

I got the feeling that he wanted to write his story, not so much to immortalize himself, but to share with others the many lessons he learned from his experiences. Perhaps this book might be an inspiration to others to better serve humanity, appreciate the history and culture of Liberia and understand the quest for intellectual excellence. His expression, "There are many people who helped me along the way; I only feel it's fair that I help others along their way," could very well testify to this.

As fate would have it, he never did finish the book due to his untimely death. I have purposely kept the manuscript as close as possible to Miah's original voice and words, with only minor edits for clarity. As a result, there are times when Miah seemingly moves between the fictional John Bowers, M.D. character and his own, personal narrative. Additionally, he did not get to write the chapters on his immediate family and I know this was his intention; therefore, I decided to include information about our life together hoping that I could say what he would have wanted to say based on our many discussions.

The book is divided into two parts: the first, the original autobiographical novel written by Henry Nehemiah Cooper, M.D. and the second, the story of our life together including the Liberian Official Gazette announcing his death, excerpts of tributes to him, a listing of some of his writings, pictorial reflections and a bibliography.

The Return of the Guinea Fowl
An Autobiographical Novel of a Liberian Doctor

Prologue

According to ancient folklore, the guinea fowl is the only wild bird of West Africa that cannot be held in captivity. Any attempt to domesticate this avian species is said to be foredoomed to failure. And, as every farm boy knows, a different sort of trap is required to capture a guinea fowl. So smart and cautious is this bird that no ordinary trap can fool him.

So, it should come as no surprise that (for a man) to be dubbed a guinea fowl is, at best, a mixed compliment. Precisely which of those attributes are being extolled? On one hand, it may be a compliment to be thought of as smart, agile and untrappable. But then how about being untamable or wild, or worse yet, having the propensity for returning to the jungle even after a full dose of literacy and Christian indoctrination?

Such is the reputation of the Gola people of Liberia. Today, they are a small tribe in the northwestern high forest region of the country. Even by West African standards, they are a small tribe, numbering perhaps less than 40,000, having assimilated into neighboring groups – principally the Vais and Mandigoes, their traditional allies over the centuries. Even so, they have preserved their uniqueness by having a language so difficult that it is said only they can speak it without flaw. No wonder—for in the Gola language there is not a single regular verb. And, a variation in pitch of a single sound can give as many as seven or eight different meanings. The Golas have also been assimilated into what represents the residual of the original settler group of so-called Americo-Liberians—the repatriated black Americans that settled the country in the early 19th century with the bold and ambitious scheme of evangelizing Africa and creating there an "asylum for the free people of color."

The story of this encounter between black men and women from two different worlds has never been told. And, it may never be told. In the wake of the recent violent revolution in Liberia, the story stands to be further distorted with time. After all, the techniques of news documentation on a worldwide scale are so new that only the culmination of 150 years of interaction are actually on record as they say, "in living color." Perhaps that is very natural, too, because only that garish and bloody climax was sensational enough to merit worldwide attention.

All previous documentation of the Liberian experiment had been limited to the quaint vignettes of the Old South-style funerals with marching bands and black men in black suits with white ties and tails, under the tropical sun, over 90 degrees, in the Amos 'n' Andy tradition. These sequences amused and entertained the American audiences for which they were filmed in the 1940s and 50s. Even then, the anachronism was appalling.

In 1980, the Amos 'n' Andy routine was not just appalling. It was not entertaining even to the intended audience. When these old film clips were deftly interspersed and spliced with new film of a series of ludicrous interviews with some unsuspecting Liberian politicians, it made a perfect incitement documentary for a volatile and shaky Liberian society, particularly at a time when the country was in the throes of economic depression. The architect of this piece of social engineering, intended or otherwise, was none other than the CBS series, "60 Minutes." In an earlier generation, only one half of this two-phased bomb would have exploded – those sympathizers in the American audience. But, in 1980, thanks to videotape home recording, the Liberian half of the bomb exploded on time—as fast as the next Pan American jet could cross the Atlantic!

Those who dispute the connection between the "60 Minutes" piece and the bloody overthrow of the Liberian government on April 12, 1980, will have no argument here. The most that anyone can objectively claim is that the "60 Minutes" program was a catalyst, a powerful catalyst beyond a doubt.

The big story is too important to be fictionalized. It must be told elsewhere. The story here is the biography of John Bowers, M.D., and it is related to the big story because John Bowers was one of those people known as guinea fowls. He was also a part of the people known as the Americo-Liberians, and more recently as the "Congo" people, against whom much of the recent propaganda of suppression of black men by black men has been directed. The passage of John Bowers from the tiny village where his grandfather's tomb is still a sacred place, through the missionary school in Monrovia, through college and medical schools in the U.S. South, on to the "great big white hospitals up North," and then back to the jungle, was eventful by any standard. And, it is a good story because it lends itself to the telling, and even to some embellishment. After all, one of his grandfathers had over seventy concubines, in addition to the prescribed four wives of Islam. The facts also show that while that grandfather was a hereditary Paramount Chief of the Gola Tribe and had 70-odd concubines, the other grandfather was a Methodist minister who was born in South Carolina in 1850. Naturally, he was allowed only one wife—at a time, that is. And it is interesting that he didn't keep that Commandment. But that is another story.

Many who read this story may believe that John Bowers, M.D. is a composite. Well, although he is not, he might well be. He is one of the unique group of black people who link the contemporary African continent with America by blood. But Dr. Bowers tells his own story.

The Guinea Fowl

My name, John Bowers, is an unlikely name for a native African, but it was honestly come by. My father's parents had been brought to Liberia as children by their parents some time in the mid 19th century. My mother, one of the 70-something children of the eminent Paramount Chief Jaa Sibi, had been taken by a missionary as a very young child and reared into a gentle lady of aristocratic bearing. She had a fine education that included nursing school at the University of Dakar and training in the hospitals of the University of Paris. She was fluent in English and French, and God knows how she retained proficiency in her native Gola, one of the most difficult of African tongues. Yet, Mama spoke this language with the skill and grace of a professional interpreter just as her father before her had been for several Liberian presidents. She was proud and she was smart.

I can remember, when as a very small boy, I was sent up country to spend time with my maternal grandmother. She was a fine old lady, who understood some rudimentary English, but who would not defile her tongue to speak a white man's language. Her only violation of this rule was when she whispered the Gola translation of a word that I might say to her in English, the only tongue I understood at age four when I was strapped to her back. With this kind of expert tutoring, I soon succumbed as kids that age will. Within a very few months, I had forgotten English and was fluent in all three of the commonly spoken dialects of the village. I stayed with Grandma and went through the initiation rites into the Poro secret male society complete with guillotine circumcision at age five. Not that I remember much of what went on at that time. Much later in life, I had redone the whole bit. Thirty or so years later, I had gone through a surprisingly familiar ceremony into the Poro, which I could not have known about other than from the first time at the tender age of five. My re-initiation left a deeper impression coming after some twenty years of formal schooling including a Medical Degree and all its implied understanding of human psychology and physiology.

Even today, I can remember snatches from the Koran, which I had begun to study at age five when Grandma took seriously Mama's consent to "give me to her." I remember the day when Papa came up country to retrieve me from the village. It was time to start school down in Monrovia. Papa seemed ten feet tall and a giant, although I would actually grow up to be the same unremarkable height, about 5'7". I remember the wisdom of Mama, who on discovery that I no longer understood English would repeat every instruction in Gola. I was soon back to speaking English.

There was nothing like an inferiority complex about being a guinea fowl. That is, there was no complex until I met my first teacher. The sole proprietor and tormentor of kids in her own one-room school, she had been probably the first female college graduate in the country. Educated she was, but why anyone as devoid of humanity and compassion as she would ever elect to be a teacher is anyone's guess. She flogged children without mercy. I can remember the occasion when, just back from the bush, I picked up a Royal Reader, upside down and went on reciting in unison with the rest of the class. When Miss Beulah discovered this transgression, her reaction was swift and to the point. She added the epithet of "guinea fowl." In my six-year-old mind, this meant a prediction that I would revert to type. Like that untamable, wild bird, I could never be educated. Unfortunately, this flogging I never forgot. Thirty years later, as a qualified specialist in surgery, I had the occasion to see Miss Beulah in her last days. She was a mere shadow of her old self. The large eroding, destructive phagedenic ulcer on her right leg had remained throughout her life as a mark of identification. Her lean face and set jaws remained as defiant as ever, but the whining, taunting voice that had tormented fully a third of my generation was now reduced to a mere whisper. I felt pity for her when I saw her in my office that day, and upon reflection, considered that perhaps she had acted in good faith all those years before. But I still found it difficult to forgive that bitter insult from so long ago. It worried me then that humans can be as unkind and unforgiving as we both had been. She by nature, I thought, and I, justifiably, despite my desire to be compassionate.

My memories of Old Beulah were not without a few humorous moments. There were some sadistic overtones, perhaps, but nevertheless capable of evoking a chuckle, even after thirty years. There was, for example, the day at school when the older boys, including my brothers, had provoked her deliberately. Old Beulah predictably pulled out a bunch of Guava branches and commanded each one in turn to stick his backside out for the prescribed punishment. With her first stroke, to the cadence of that whining, tormenting voice, and with a half grin on her bony face, showing her single gold-capped tooth, she relished the scream of anguish she produced in the course of making mincemeat of some youngster's ass. Suddenly, on this particular day, there was pandemonium in the one-room school. Jack, her prey of the moment, had squirmed loose and with the precision of a professional footballer, had delivered a swift barefoot kick directly on that old, incurable ulcer on her right leg. After that, school was out for the day and we laughed like hell all the way home at the thought of scoring one against the old witch. All of the merciless floggings that followed during the next two years, I thought, were contrived to avenge that single day when she had gotten a taste of her own medicine.

Then there was the memory of the day she had beaten the hell out of my brother, Sam, all across the face, and he had come home screaming with sweat and blood and tears mingled. The injury hadn't been severe, as it happened, but with three of us screaming bloody murder, Papa had been incensed. He, no doubt, felt the urge to show his boys that he was their hero. He had bolted out of the back door with a loaded shotgun, swearing loudly that this was Old Beulah's last day on earth. We had all felt pride swelling in us and a premature joy at the prospect of our tormentor's comeuppance. But, Papa had stalled just long enough in the backyard, repeating his threats with an ever-increasing crescendo. Mama, cool and quiet, as usual, had paid the old man no mind. She was busy inspecting Sam's face and efficiently applying a cold compress. When after several moments Papa was still less than five yards from the door, she looked out and ever so slightly raised her voice, "Charlie." She said nothing more. The old man turned around, came in and stood that old cap gun in the corner swearing that a major catastrophe had just been averted. Then he swore that this would be the last, positively the last goddamned time that he would be dissuaded from what he knew was his duty to his children. Mama only smiled. She knew her Charlie for what he was. He wouldn't have shot a mouse in anger. We were, nonetheless, appeased. Papa had stood up for us. Papa, too, was proud that he had had this little tantrum. Perhaps he even felt big and bad. That day, to us, he was big and bad. Over the years, however, we came to know the truth. Mama could handle her man with nothing more than a grunt of disgust or just by sucking her teeth—that strange and wordless gesture which among Africans has a thousand meanings. It can mean anything from disbelief to defiance or just plain dismissal as in, "Who the hell are you kidding?"

Old Beulah lived out her days, and when I heard she had died, it made no impression, thank God. I had been worried that I might feel happy to hear of Old Beulah's death, but I wasn't. I wasn't sad either. I felt absolutely nothing. It was just one of the millions of events that happen. People dying, babies being born, rain falling.

I only attended Miss Beulah's school for two years, but God, it seemed like a lifetime. After that, it was time to move on to the school run by the white missionaries where I would remain all the way through high school.

Christian Union Academy

The school had been there for over 100 years. Proud of tradition, it was older than the republic itself. The name, Christian Union Academy, denoted all the pride of being the oldest foreign mission of the church. It was the Christian white man's gift to the heathen, an effort to bring Christendom to darkest Africa. It didn't matter that they had produced less than a hundred high school graduates in a hundred years. After all, almost everybody who was anybody had gotten whatever education they had from CUA. And, in all fairness, one had to admit that a ninth grade education in 1909 must have been a hell of a lot superior to a B.A. in 1969, or so it seemed anyway. Those old grads had read all the classics, knew Latin and Greek, and had committed quite a bit of the Bible to memory. On top of that, after so many years you knew all four verses of all the standard Methodist hymns.

The Academy had a proud tradition of having always had a white missionary as Principal. The white folks in America must have thought a lot of these niggers. These were their special niggers. All the ravages of malaria and dysentery that had spelled almost certain death for missionaries, who ventured out there, had not been enough to discourage the church. They had persisted through the years. In fact, it said right there on the stained glass window in the new auditorium, "Although a thousand may die, never give up on Africa." Those were the dying words of a young missionary, Melvin B. Cox, who had given up his life way back in the 1830s when he had been sent to start the school. One cannot help but feel sympathy for the nobility of purpose of such people. Especially when you consider them as contemporaries of the slave masters of the American South and constituents of statesmen like old Senator John C. Calhoun. It is difficult to ascertain whether the story is true, but somewhere it was said that Calhoun's solution to the problem of the Black man in America was to truss them up in sacks and dump them into the Atlantic. His estimate of their value was that they would not be worth the bubbles that would issue from their mass drowning. With sentiments like those around, it must have taken a lot of guts or compassion or something to come to Africa to stay in those days. Chances are that man's minds and motives were not much different in 1830 from what they were in 1930, or what they will be in 2030, for that matter.

Missionaries had come and gone. Some had died; others had lived to write of their experiences, real and imagined. Some had remained, until the end, faithful servants of their God, loving the people as much as anybody can love anybody else. Many, though, were condescending and self-righteously serving their sentence among the heathen to assure themselves a seat at the Right Hand on Judgment Day.

I stayed on through high school at the Academy. As was the practice, one out of every four in a family went to school free of charge. It was sound economics for Mama to designate me as the free one; after all, I seemed to present the least hazard of flunking out at the time. I watched successive waves of missionaries come and go. By the time I got to the Academy, hardly anyone died of malaria and dysentery anymore. There was quinine and Atabrine by then, and by the 1940s, there were also improved conditions of service that allowed regular furloughs for recuperation in the temperate climates. Years later, air conditioning, antibiotics, jet travel, telephones, and even television—all had made life less sacrificial and much more bearable for missionaries as well as everyone else.

With the coming of the Second World War, though, there were some lapses in recruitment of dedicated self-sacrificing souls. This must have been the only explanation for some of the more colorful characters that were sent to bring light unto the darkness. There was, for example, the young Ph.D. from California, who served his three years. A dapper Clark Gable type with a French wife, an accomplished pianist. They had gone back to the States some years later and collaborated on one of those mocking bestsellers that laughed at Africa and the people they had gone to serve.

Then, there was the Arkansas cowboy, already over the hill when he got to Africa. After an Army career in the Philippines and Siam, he spoke Tagalog fluently and regaled us with stories of his exploits in the Far East. For some reason, the only stories that stuck in the mind were those of natives rushing about and the wanton killings of "Huramentado" those Muslim marauders of the Island of Mindanao. The cowboy had a gentle wife and two youngsters; one of the same age as I was. I can remember Mrs. Cowboy's expression when she first met Mama. "Why, we sure think as much of J.B. as you do," she had said. When Mama raised an eyebrow, Mrs. Cowboy had retreated, adding, "Well, almost as much as you do." She must have thought much of me, for she used to have me spend weekends with the family, sharing the bed with Junior. Of course, this was no big deal at the time; we didn't even know where Arkansas was much less that we weren't supposed to be as good as them. The missionaries had told us that God was love and we were all God's children, and we believed it. Even if there were subtle Jim Crowisms, which of us could have recognized it at that time? That is still one of the strangest phenomena – racism American-style. Only after years in the American South, could I recognize in retrospect, the meaning of some of the innocent encounters of my childhood. It required a special sensitivity to detect some of the petty apartheid that was native to the U.S. of that era. The same may be true today, but things have been so modified that my children draw absolutely different conclusions from the same encounters today.

There was that Saturday morning when Cowboy Junior and I had been playing with toy soldiers. Boom! Junior's troops had wiped out my forces. Patiently, I regrouped my soldiers and Boom! The African army had ambushed Junior's men. In a rage, Junior had demanded that the scene be replayed. Whoever heard of an African army, with cannons, ambushing the American army? "Take it back!" he screamed. "Take it back!" When I refused, I suddenly found myself engaged in what was the most savage brawl I had encountered up to that point in life. Biting, kicking, head butting, no holds barred. At the bell, that is when Mrs. Cowboy intervened, her Junior was very much on the short end. More bloodied, lip busted, t-shirt shredded. Mrs. Cowboy made us both come into the living room and sit on the floor at her feet. She lectured us on sportsmanship, and then ordered a tall glass of ice-cold Coca-Cola for each of us before she began to read to us.

At that moment, in walked the old Cowboy himself. One look at Junior's face and he demanded, "What the hell happened?" No missionary ever used language like that, I thought. Junior started to cry all over again and related the events for his daddy, carefully omitting his act of aggression. The old Cowboy picked up a chair and started at me, then age twelve. "You God-damned nigger. I'll fix you!" he cried. Mrs. Cowboy caught the chair in mid-air, pushed the old man aside and embraced junior and me, weeping. She said a little prayer out loud and told us that God didn't want people to behave like Daddy. She prayed for Daddy, too, asking God to tame his violent temper. She also told us that nobody should be abused for being black or white. I have wondered, since that time, which of this pair was the missionary and which just came along for the ride. I later discovered a secret that almost nobody outside the missionary community had known. The old Cowboy daily belted at least a pint of Bourbon and many of his frequent rages were nothing more than acute alcoholic intoxication. At the end of this episode, Junior and I remained friends until the family departed for home.

Many years later and after several minor encounters with gas station attendants and Georgia cops, I began to understand why I never did get a letter from Junior as he had promised, and also why the family had not given me their address at home when they left. I could also understand one document that had puzzled me. The night before the Cowboy family left Africa, I had innocently gone up to daddy Cowboy and asked, "Please give me a recommendation." This was a typical fashion of everybody who worked for foreigners at the time. I had been an errand boy in their mission office for two years. Certainly a recommendation stating I had been honest, hard working and reliable might have been a valuable testimonial to show the succeeding missionary family. The old man, when he discovered that this young black boy was persistent, had scrawled this note on a plain piece of paper, "This is to certify that this boy has worked for me and the Academy for two years. I recommend him to anybody who wants a boy to work." No name, no date, not even on the Academy's letterhead! I was crushed, dismayed and puzzled, but somehow, not bitter. The old man was just tired, I thought. Maybe I should have pointed out to him that the testimonial was unsigned, but anyway, I knew I couldn't use it. Even at age fourteen, I recognized the worthlessness of that piece of paper. What I couldn't figure out was why he had done that. Such is the innocence and naiveté of unconditioned youth.

To complete the list of "Bwana" type missionaries, there was the old professor who had spent many years in Africa. He was a pious, old, red-faced preacher. He couldn't stand to hear certain hymns sung with out weeping. In fact, he so loved Jesus that at the very sound of

His name, he would choke. He cried so much, three or four times a week during the daily chapel services, that when he didn't cry we figured the services had been profane. This was the same preacher who later left Liberia with his pretty, hazel-eyed, brown–skinned secretary, whom he had stolen from her young husband. We never learned whether the Mission Board took any action or even heard of it. She was certainly fine enough to be seduced by any red-blooded man. Nobody thought about missionaries as ordinary worldly men. Passion? What was that? Not for these saints, we thought.

On the other side of the ledger, there was the articulate Yale man, a dead ringer for Billy Graham, whose erudite sermons and scholarly lectures in Economics were unsurpassed by any I had ever heard. The candor and forthrightness of this man had gotten him into trouble with the local big wheels many times. He never backed down. In fact, it was at one of these showdowns with the authorities that I was to have my first experience with bucking the establishment. The Yale man had been accused of slandering the state and the Negro race by saying, during an Anthropology class, that Africans made human sacrifices. He had not precisely said that. But, a disgruntled student who had flunked out said that he had, and that required a high-level Government investigation. I, by then a typist and all-around office boy, was called as a witness.

The Board had met, and the hot, muggy library was in a hushed silence. Not less than three government cabinet ministers were members of the Board and they were all there in their cravats and woolen suits, sweating and fanning themselves. "Harrumph!" The Secretary of Education had cleared his throat before reading the charges. This was a clear case of "persona non grata" in the making. Before calling me to testify, however, one of the other official gentlemen had benevolently begun to lecture me on the impropriety and utter arrogance of standing before my elders with my hands in my pockets. "Take your hands out of your pockets and answer the questions." "Did you or did you not hear the Yale man say, etc.etc..." I responded in an even voice, "Gentlemen, you invited me here. YOU are asking ME for a statement. I cannot see how the position of my hands should affect what I have to say. And, in any case, I think it is you who have insulted me, not I who have disrespected you. Now, for your question..." I was not allowed to continue. "Get out!" one shouted. "Leave immediately," said another. Before leaving, I heard the Secretary of Education say, "You're never going to amount to anything!" I was ushered out of the Board Room and so never heard the rest of the proceedings, but the Yale man stayed on. I can only guess at how the proceedings went on.

Another memory of the Yale man was his offer of a daring experiment to prove to us, once and for all, the fallacy of believing in ghosts. We had all seen pallbearers staggering around in circles as they proceeded towards the grave with an unwilling corpse. Such struggles would become increasingly more pronounced as the casket came nearer to individuals attending the funeral who were suspected of foul play. The greater the struggle, the more potent the spirit within the casket was thought to be. The Yale man could get no "takers" when he proposed to be the fourth pallbearer with three of us as volunteers to prove that dead bodies had no such power.

Another of this new breed of modern missionary, was the young chap, barely out of college, who had come; first, to fill the unexpired term of an older, departing missionary, then stayed on. He was soft spoken and unpretentious, one of the few truly devout and humble men I would ever meet. Where the Yale man was confident, even brash, this chap was diffident and shy. His English-born wife was no less dedicated, and perhaps even a bit smarter than he was. The two made a lasting impression on me as a young man. Years later in the U.S. South, when I had been almost convinced that the solution to all the ills of society lay in killing every redneck cracker (new terms in my vocabulary at the time), the thought of this couple stood out in bold contradiction to the idea that all white people are evil. There are some good white folk, and, some missionaries who went to Africa were people of God. This young couple had asked the church Board to send me a check of five dollars every month from their meager salary throughout my college career.

The aging parents of this shy missionary had come through Georgia en route to Florida during my first semester of college. They planned to stop over to visit me, a former student of their son in Africa. Being natives of the U.S. West Coast, they really didn't know the score down South. The first hitch was when they discovered that I could not stay with them or visit them at their segregated trailer park. The Dean of Students at my college tactfully offered them parking space on the campus and a room in the guest suite of the dormitory. They graciously accepted. On a Sunday afternoon, driving across town with my roommate and me, the old couple was refused service at three gas stations. My roommate, the young black American, solved the problem that had puzzled the old couple from the West and the young African immigrant. He said, "Pull over to the curb, Ma'am. Now, you and Pops get in the back seat, and J.B. will ride up front with me. Don't you worry, Ma'am? I've got a chauffeur's license, and I can manage the trailer." As we pulled into the next service station, the blond attendant literally sprinted to the car. "Yes, sir. What can we do for you today? Fill 'er up? How's the weather out West? Nice day, isn't it? Thank you, sir. Come see us again soon, hear?"

What was to account for this effusive display of Southern hospitality? As any two year-old in the South in 1947 knew, the difference was in the seating arrangement. The old white couple in the back seat was probably going south for winter with their two nigger servants. One was the chauffeur, the other, probably, the valet. They had to be rich folks. Certainly, they were deserving of the best attentions of any "peckerwood" boy in a gas station. The earlier arrangement, with me seated beside Miss Anne up front, and the old man back there with another nigger laughing and talking, was too much for a self-respecting Southerner. Visions of miscegenation were conjured up; niggers raping white women, and all such happenings that these do-gooders bring on themselves by messing around with niggers. Any "sensible" white man, at that time, "knew" that niggers needed to stay in their places.

Still another variant of missionary types was an older lady at CUA, Miss Sally Mather. I never could figure her out. She was a life-long spinster who had raised a number of African children as her own. They called her Mommy, and for all anyone knew, she loved them as her own. But, somehow, she never did seem to take to me. I had heard her laying me out to the Yale man once. She said I was arrogant, disrespectful, and really not much good. The Yale man had said in hushed tones in the back office, "He's a good kid, Sally." The rest, I didn't hear, and I never let on that I had heard anything at all. The Yale man must have been convincing. Two years after graduating from the Academy while working as office clerk, bookkeeper and even pinch-hitting as a teacher of Latin, Algebra and World History, it was time to try to get a scholarship to go to college in the U.S. I already had an offer from a small Negro college for a $100 tuition scholarship, provided that I could get to Atlanta, Georgia to take advantage of it. Two years' savings from salaries like those paid by the Academy fell far short of plane fare. Miss Sally came through with the final $100. She had said that $50 was an outright gift, and $50 was a loan to be repaid, without interest, at any time in the future. As things turned out, I was out of hock by the end of the first semester. Two janitor jobs at $12 each in the men's dormitory, waiting tables on the weekends at the Jewish Progressive Club, and making side bets on the weekend crap games in the basement made that very easy.

But, counting up for the plane fare wasn't nearly as easy as I am making it sound. My aggregate savings, salted away over a period of two years came to $240. Hell, that was real thrift. At $20 a month, the total earnings had been just over $400 in a little less than two years. That had only been possible because I also moonlighted at teaching night school. The $10 salary from that job came through as often as not. Then, there was the little Combo I played the clarinet in at local dances. Sometimes we collected the fee in cash, sometimes in kind. Like the Fourth of July party given by the American Embassy staff. The band was paid one case of duty-free Canadian Club whiskey and all the beer we could drink. That was when I discovered that boilermakers don't go down too well. Six beers and a fifth of Canadian Club left me, as close to being comatose as I have ever been. Chipping in with the family budget, and supporting my newly acquired smoking habit at two packs per week, plus an occasional GI beer on the black market had taken up the rest of my income. Of course, I didn't have to drink beer. One could always get high on the local rum. But that was low class. At five cents a shot, it was too cheap and the odor was betraying, besides. A guy could easily lose the respect of his peers by drinking stuff like that. At seventeen, we didn't really want to get drunk. Just to let people see us drinking was kicks enough.

The Yale man had worked with a sharp pencil. Suppose we raise you to $25. That would give you $100 more for the twenty months. That would make it $340." Not enough, so how about $30. Four hundred and forty dollars, still not enough. Well, up to $40; back raise you to $40 and we've got over $600; but no. How could we justify that when the highest salary on the faculty was $40?" So, we settled on

$35. Back-raising my salary to $35 a month produced an extra $300 for a grand total of $540, by the grace of God. With Miss Sally's $100, that was $640. The plane fare was $635. Passing the hat among the family provided the margin of an extra $50 to travel with. We had it made. Academics were no sweat. I had graduated with honors and had been tutored during the two years since graduation in English and the art of taking American-style multiple-choice examinations. The Yale man's wife was a first-class teacher, so I was all set for college.

Teeta

As eager as I was to get to the U.S. and start my college education, I knew there would be things I would miss about home. But, a particular loss at a young age, had made me sure that I wanted to become among the best doctors anywhere. And that meant I needed a solid education.

We lived on Snapper Hill in Monrovia, Liberia. At fourteen, Teeta was a plump, round-faced, slightly stoop-shouldered little girl. The normal events of her adolescence were progressing neither precociously nor, by any means, retarded. She had begun to acquire breasts, of which she was alternately embarrassed and proud. I knew this because she had told me so. She was a pretty child, with a copper complexion of virtually flawless velvety skin, the precise color that those who are paler strive to get by tanning and those who are darker frequently try to attain by bleaching.

Her full head of hair was never black, although she thought it should be, and was angered when the other little girls in the neighborhood mocked her and called her "red head." Her hair was not red, either. It was actually of a reddish-brown hue that blended perfectly with the color of her face. The downy baby hair at her temples that marked her hairline blended invisibly with her profile.

Her eyebrows were slightly darker and naturally arched over her deep-set but large eyes, which were covered by expressive lids bearing the most luxuriant brush of eyelashes. When she was happy and laughed, her eyes literally danced, revealing pale brown irises through the natural squint that she affected because of her near-sightedness. She had an abrupt little nose, on the crest of which she habitually perspired. She would grin faintly and protest when people told her that people who sweat on their noses were mean. She hardly needed to protest. She was shy, yes. Quiet, taciturn, yes. Almost to a fault with strangers. But not mean. She couldn't even hold her own in an argument with other little girls in the neighborhood. She literally ran away if anyone spoke in too loud a voice.

When scolded, she was submissive enough, but never effusive or very demonstrative in her affection. She suffered silently in physical pain, but dissolved in tears at an insult. Insults were frequent since the other kids always called her "blind bat" when she removed the thick lenses she had to wear. And, when she didn't remove them, the children laughed at her glasses. So, she stayed mostly to herself and a few trusted friends who were, in fact, enough company for her.

We all called her "Teeta." That was the baby talk translation for "sister" a name that had stuck from infancy. One of four sisters in the family, she was a natural model for the younger girls. For the same reason, she was a special pet for the older boys. For Mama, of course, she was a sort of Good Luck Charm. After all, it was she who had broken the "spell." There had been a succession of boys born into this family before Teeta. After the first boy, each succeeding new arrival— they had occurred with almost seasonal regularity—was awaited with an urgency and anticipation that defied explanation. In those hard and lean days of the Depression, a man's riches were his children. The size of his family somehow denoted how many times God had blessed him. It didn't matter that with each succeeding blessing it became more difficult to keep body and soul together. Those were the days before the "pill." And, from a practical viewpoint, it made good sense to have as many children as one could if one wanted to be assured that a few would survive into adulthood. The "spasms," plus Blackwater Fever, Black Measles and "Open Mole" took a frightful toll on babies born in the community. The toll was even more frightful in the bush country, where the natives had a simpler explanation of the works of nature. Each family would give its statistics on the number of children by stating how many had been born and how many "went back," that is died at various points of infancy.

My family had been one of the luckiest. We never had to say how many had gone back. In fact, none had gone back. Mama, a trained nurse, as was sufficiently aware and able to recognize illnesses for what they were. She also knew that fevers should be respected and not taken as an inevitable consequence of existence. Most of all, she didn't subscribe to the native theory that children should not be fed during daylight hours lest they become too noisy and unmanageable. But, what was most rare, for that era, was the fact that Mama knew about nutritional elements and could discover them in the most unlikely species of wild roots and leaves. She could prepare a remarkable variety of filling meals that cost almost nothing. She was a "boss scavenger" that kept her brood well filled. Whatever toxins there may have been in those exotic diets didn't have a chance to do us harm. Mama was also a skilled therapist in the use of vermifuges and assorted purgatives. These potions were administered with the regularity and consistency that only a cardiac clinic could surpass. I knew the potions so well that I could close my eyes and recreate the noxious odors and tastes on command. The most despised flavor was the worm expellant.

There must have been therapeutic value in those potions, and Mama's skill was unquestionable. In fact, she was an outstanding success in raising her four boys and the succeeding four girls without loss—without loss, that is, until we lost Teeta, everybody's pet. There were many aspects of that loss that made it harder to accept or explain, and consequently, made the hurt so deep and lingering. For Mama, life was never to be the same. She wept each time somebody she knew lost a child. That was all the similarity necessary. If somebody's child drowned or died in an automobile accident, she wept for them because the accidental death reminded her of how unexpected our loss of Teeta had been. If somebody's child had been severely ill or even died of an incurable and wasting disease, she wept for them just as bitterly, because it reminded her of how desperately ill Teeta had been for all of forty-eight hours, and of how helpless the doctors had seemed when she had called them.

Teeta might as well have had an incurable disease. The two doctors in town had come in, gone out, returned again and again, given injections; large injections, small injections. They had rubbed her with various greases, made her drink various potions; they had bound her plump, brown, finely-chiseled face with all manner of leaves, and doused her thick locks of reddish brown hair with cold water, hot water, and had done just about everything that helpless, poor people could do to save a child they didn't want to lose. Among the helpers and volunteers, there were, inevitably, the occultists. Those who cut cards, those who "could see", those who dreamed straight and those who, invariably, dreamed backwards. Those who had a secret to tell provided they would not be given away. Those who knew WHO had done this terrible thing. In our culture, there is always a mixture of people around. Even today, NOBODY ever dies of natural causes in Liberia. If he drowns, he was sold to the water people. And if it isn't the water people, then it is some other kind of people. And there is always someone who benefits from the sale. If the alleged beneficiary is obviously prosperous, no further explanation is needed. That is how he got his wealth. If he is an obvious failure in life, then THAT is why he has failed. He is evil. Hardest to explain, however, is the beneficiary who is just average. He is usually then reputed to have some hidden wealth or THAT (the selling of innocent victims) is the reason why he hasn't yet made it. It is a no-win, foolproof theory of life and death.

Fortunately, Mama never believed that Teeta was either sold or witched or poisoned. There had been several candidates –"envious or self-serving relatives"- who were proposed as vendors. They had all been proposed by people who "could see." This business of "seeing" is probably one of the most debilitating neuroses on the African continent. In one form or another, it probably is epidemic among black people worldwide.

I can remember my faint disgust that day, over thirty years ago, when Teeta died. I had overheard one of those people who "could see" as she whispered to Mama that I "could see." She had made the diagnosis of my clairvoyance just by looking at me. She had seen something that made her know that we were both seers. Just what it was, I didn't know. All I knew was that I had not seen a damned thing about Teeta's illness. If I had, I certainly would have said something. Teeta had been my closest pal, and if I had seen anything coming to take her away, I was sure that whatever it was would have had to take us both that day. When Mama held me close to her bosom and asked, "Did you see this coming, Grandpa?" (She had nicknamed me

"Grandpa" because she said I had always seemed older than my years.) Our tears mingled as I sobbed for the first and only time during this tragedy. Mama had felt my unspoken denial in the rhythms with which my thin body vibrated with an almost unbearable grief. If there is anything such as a moment when one makes a decision, that must have been it for me. Certainly, in one of the moments in that long 48-hour ordeal when Teeta lay dying, I had committed myself to the work that would become my life. It was not merely that I decided to become a doctor. I had always said I would be a doctor. But it was the moment when I knew with complete certainty that I MUST become a doctor.

I could not have known all the theories and psychological concepts of what shaped motives and attitudes, but I did know that if there was anybody I understood, or anybody who understood me, if there was anybody who would do anything for me, or anybody for whom I would do ANYTHING, if there was anybody who could forgive or explain away any mistake I could make, or anybody whose mistakes I could forgive without question, or whose every fault I could explain with sympathy, I knew for sure that if there were such a person, it was Teeta. Teeta and I had grown up especially close. I was younger than the other boys. Not that much younger. But they never let me forget that they were my betters. I could not run as fast; I could not throw rocks with as much force or precision; I was clumsy. I could never keep up when they were walking across town to Grandma's house. And, if I went along, they could never heckle any of the street beggars or assorted cripples and make a clean getaway. They could never get away, that is, unless they left me to get caught. And if I got caught, I was too innocent to lie. I would surely say who I was, and then they could be traced. So my older brothers were sure to make me miserable enough so that I stayed away from them if for no other reason than self-preservation. Whenever that urge diminished in me, one of the older boys made the point more directly. They either kicked me, wringed my floppy ears or did any one of several acts of minor torture to me that insured my disappearance.

On the other hand, I was Teeta's hero. Although she was basically quiet and withdrawn, she was pleasant to talk to. She had worn glasses since she was five years old when a teacher had decided that she was either dumb or blind. She had been fitted with very thick lenses to correct myopia and suddenly transformed into a whiz kid who completed two grades in a year. But she tired easily. And once night came, even with correcting glasses, the kerosene lamps were never adequate for her to read with comfort. When night came, I was her eyes. I read to her. I helped her to do the long addition problems in her homework. I read lessons and I also read books that were not textbooks. I signed out books from the Academy library to read to her. Books in which I had no particular interest but that she had heard her girlfriends at the convent school talk about. She would remember the titles and the authors to tell me. In the evenings, when I returned from the marketplace where I sold homemade bread, I would read the stories to her; together we would change the endings of the stories, making up an endless stream of fantasies. We never tired of each other's company, it seemed. We shared each other's confidence to a degree not common between brother and sister. For instance, when Teeta was somewhere between eleven and twelve years old and had noted the first signs of beginning to menstruate, it was to me she had run and whispered. I, at fourteen, was as educated in the matter as anybody she knew. I had assured her that it was a natural phenomenon and had advised that she consult Mama about what to do.

In a relationship like ours, it was easy to understand why I had had a confused and bewildered reaction to her untimely and sudden death. Thirty years later, the entire sequence remained vivid in my mind. In fact, up until a certain point, it seemed that my pursuit of a medical career was an unconscious pursuit of an explanation for Teeta's death.

The first time a woman brought her twelve-year-old daughter into my office screaming and delirious, I had casually recommended hospitalization at the Government Hospital. " I am a surgeon, Madam. And this is a case of Convulsions due to the Fever... most likely malaria. Take her to the hospital right away." The lady had said thanks and was on her way out of the door when I remembered how helpless Mama had been on that day that Teeta lay dying. Of course, there was a difference. With Teeta, there had been only two doctors in town. In fact, there was only one real doctor. The other fellow everybody called "doctor," but everybody knew he wasn't really a doctor. He was some sort of a dresser or nurse; but being a foreigner, having an accent, and with nobody knowing whose son or grandson he was, the people had taken his word for it: he had said he was a doctor. Moreover, what choice was there? He had cured some people who had been desperately ill. So, for talking purposes, there were two doctors for Teeta. But by the time the lady with the sick girl came into my office, there were perhaps thirty doctors in town. And any self-respecting, first-class specialist in surgery would hardly consider himself an expert in treating malaria. At least that was the way I had formulated my thoughts after fifteen years of study in America.

Suddenly I remembered how Teeta was delirious, and how she had cried and groaned and begged for water, and how she had imagined ants crawling on the wall... just like this little girl who attracted the morbid attention of the people seated in the crowded waiting room. Before I knew it, I had shouted. "Come back, Ma! Bring her here. Let us see what it is before you go to the hospital." Back in the treatment room, the urine sample had been BLACK, JET BLACK, just like Teeta's urine had been. I knew what it was - hemoglobinuria[1]; and I knew what had to be done. No leaves or grease or hot or cold water. Not in this day and age. I had started an intravenous drip of dextrose in Normal saline, to which I added chloroquin phosphate. Then, I took her over to the old Government Hospital and wrote orders myself.

I stopped by each day before going home and saw her. I had ordered the nurses to keep a record of intake and output, and I had ordered electrolyte studies. The older hands around only snickered. They had never seen so much fuss over a simple case of Blackwater Fever. The laboratory wasn't yet doing electrolytes. In fact, they did well if they gave you a simple CBC or complete blood count. But I had been home for only a few weeks and didn't know any better. Furthermore, the staff said that whenever people were brought in this late with Blackwater Fever, there was no use. Death was a certain outcome. I hadn't the experience they had with this problem, but I knew too much about physiology to accept that degree of fatalism. What the old Government Hospital staff did not realize was that this was a very personal matter for me. This was the reason why I had gone through medical school to begin with. This was also the reason why I

---

[1] Hemoglobinuria, as defined by Wikipedia.com, "is a condition in which the oxygen transport protein hemoglobin is found in abnormally high concentrations in the urine." Source: Wikipedia contributors, "Hemoglobinuria," Wikipedia.com (accessed December 19, 2010). In malaria this occurs because red blood cells break down after being invaded by the protozoan parasites.

had come back here, to this "backwater," although it was not always in the forefront of my consciousness. It was an ever-present testimony, a soliloquy when the chips were down.

The child recovered and went home. Teeta had been avenged. In fact, over time, Teeta was avenged many times. I had heard her anguished cries of thirst in every dehydrated child I saw on the pediatric wards in America, from Mound Bayou, Mississippi to New York City. I had seen her parched lips and her trembling little body in every patient who shivered, whether it was due to septicemia or a transfusion reaction. Whenever I had occasion to reassure a frightened child, I could hear, in my mind, Teeta's plaintive cry from that awful day so many years before, "Bubba, don't let them take me, hear? Bubba, you won't let me die, will you...Bubba, please hold my head...Bubba I'm soooo HOT! Bubba, why is God making me hurt so?" On that awful day, there was nothing I could do but hold Teeta's head and mop her brow with the damp rag they used for a washcloth. Her head was hot; I remembered. When she cried in pain, I had buried my face against her cheek and cried with her. When the doctor had come to give one of those big injections, they always pushed me out; but as soon as they left, I came back and held her hand or her head, or just kneeled by the little iron bed that shook as she trembled. She reached over and hugged me around the neck and whispered, "Bubba, I'm gonna die.... Bubba, I know you're sorry for me." Everything she said to me when I was at her side, made sense; yet, whenever I left the room and we heard her cries from outside, they sounded like the incoherent babbling of psychotic patients in distress. How could she make so much sense when I was next to her and babble psychotically from a distance? I thought that there must have been some special bond between us that made her lucid when she spoke to me and only to me. I had stayed home from school both days that she was ill. I could not have gone. I would not have been able to think of anything if I had. I would only have heard her cries for me to come back.

On her final day, when she lay almost comatose, weakened by fever and sheer exhaustion of rigors, and undoubtedly, quieted by the merciful providence of cerebral edema and anoxia, she had died in peace. Her last audible words had been, "Bubba, I'm tired... never mind...I'm so tired." After that, her lips moved, but their utterance would forever remain a secret, even from me, her pal, and confidante.

For me, this was the beginning of a lifelong quest. Considering the mores of my people, it was unusual that I did not attend the funeral. I ran away from home for the next two days, wandering at night until I would fall asleep somewhere - anywhere. I hid myself during the day in the belfry of the Academy. I just lay there doing nothing in particular. Not reading, not thinking, not afraid of her ghost. In fact, I didn't even believe in ghosts. If there were ghosts, Teeta's ghost would not be one to be afraid of. Strangely, Mama never questioned my unusual behavior or disappearance. She never said so but I guess she understood why I could not have handled the additional ordeal of wake-keeping, followed by a funeral, complete with all the shrieking and recitative mourning that form a part of the ritual over the dead in our culture.

Many years later, when I got married, Mama thought I had picked the girl because she was Teeta's favorite friend at the convent school. In those two awful days of dying, in delirium, she had called the names of most of her playmates, but had been particularly insistent about the girl that I married some ten years later. There was, of course, no conscious connection between the circumstances, but Mama always thought there was, and perhaps, that was one additional reason why my wife was among Mama's favorite daughters-in-law.

The Voyage

Leaving Liberia to attend college, the voyage to the United States was an epic in itself. There were always rumors of ships due into the Monrovia seaport that came two or three weeks late and some that never came at all. When they did come, there was the problem of getting a berth. The passenger accommodations on freighters were always limited and then, there were always higher priority passengers, it seemed. The quickest way to the U.S. was by the Pan American flights that left two or three times a month. A less reliable and chancier mode of travel was by one of the U.S. Air Transport Command flights. They would accommodate civilians and important government officials whenever there were seats. Their main mission was ferrying military personnel from the North African and South European theaters, however. After the military personnel, there were the American citizens, who were stranded or on their way home on leave from service in Africa. After them, the Liberian Government officials who were traveling on official business were taken on. On down the line the priorities went, until the ubiquitous classification of "others" came up. So, it was a real stroke of luck when there were finally two available seats aboard one of these flights in early September 1946. A buddy and I, another kid on the way to college in the U.S., got the chance. It wasn't quite clear to me how I had gotten the break. Maybe Hank's parents or somebody who knew somebody had gotten us on. I was sure my folks didn't know anybody who could have swung that deal. At any rate, we did get on with the planeload of GIs from North Africa, who had stopped by the U.S. Army airstrip in Liberia to refuel. And thus began one of the most dramatic chapters in my life.

The route was from Monrovia out and down to St. Helena, a bleak mass of rocks in the South Atlantic, where there was another airstrip. We spent the night there; the next day we would cross over to the eastern coast of South America, stopping at Natal, Brazil. There was a U.S. military installation there, and that was the end of the Air Transport Command flight. The plane would continue on to the U.S., entering at some East Coast airport, but in those days of priority, there were many more people to join the flight in Natal. So, the GIs and the Government officials and the higher priority people continued on from Brazil to the U.S. The "others" had to make diverse arrangements from that point on.

It was never clear to us, these two stringy lads from West Africa, what was really happening. But then, at eighteen, never having traveled anywhere outside of the old hometown, it didn't seem to matter now that we were in this cavernous dormitory on the U.S. air base in Natal, waiting for what, we didn't know. When were we leaving? Who said we were leaving? What did the tickets say? Who had the tickets? Somebody had taken our tickets when we landed at Natal. We just followed the signs. We went down a hallway, turned right and there was a line of military personnel, which we joined because it seemed the only reasonable thing to do. Where were they going? Who knew? Soon, we were directed to another line where we were fingerprinted, required to fill out some forms, and given dog tags our names having been stamped out on the spot. Three burly noncommissioned officers at the front of the line issued soap; two green fatigue suits and a kit containing some desiccated biscuits and assorted nuts. Finally, we were presented with a key with a barracks number on it.

We continued to follow the line in what appeared a routine procedure. There were several other guys who apparently knew no more than we did, and we all simply proceeded across a dusty path arriving at a temporary building labeled "C". Well, the tag on the key said, "C", so this must be the place. The black soldier at the desk said, "Hi fellows, what's cooking? Where you cats from?" "West Africa," we responded. "West Africa, Hell. You mean Africa, South Carolina? Okay man, you can piss in my face and tell me it's raining. Ha. Ha. Ha." He laughed heartily, and waved us in. Hank and I sat there looking at each other, wondering what the hell was going on. Two green kids from Africa in the middle somewhere, knowing nothing about where or how or why we were there. We knew we were on the way to America; of course, we were on the way to America. We also knew that we had better hang on to our passports and since the Sergeant had explicitly said to wear the damned dog tags around your neck at all times, we did. There was no problem in carrying out simple orders like that. Munching on those stale biscuits and peanuts, we wondered what would happen next.

Inside of the kit with the biscuits and nuts there was a little booklet, perforated, stamped out in three sections, about 30 pages. The sections were labeled very plainly, "breakfast," "dinner," "supper," respectively. What the hell did this mean? Coupons for meals obviously. But why so many of them and who was going pay for it? The U.S. Army? Would we be expected to pay them back? Maybe we'd better not use these coupons, we reasoned. We might find out later that we didn't have enough money to pay for them.

The big, black soldier with the single stripe chevron on his arm had dropped by our room for a chat. "Hey man, where the hell'd you guys say you from?" "Liberia, West Africa." "Oh come on, man. Who you kidding? Liberia, Mississippi, my ass." And then he convulsed with laughter. "Come on, now. Don't shit me. What outfit you with?" "No outfit, man. Seriously. We're from Liberia. L-I-B-E-R-I-A." When he saw that we weren't joking; he sat on the bed inspecting the three handmade gold chains that hung around Hank's neck mingled with his new dog tag. Studying them, he was finally convinced. "What's that, man? Real gold?" "Yep" "You guys sho nuff from Africa? Well, I'll be goddamned. What the hell you doing here?" "We don't know. The Army plane brought us in and the people out there gave us all this stuff and said to come this way." "No shit?" "No, for true." Suddenly, the big fellow was in deep thought. He spoke in rapid-fire, jive language Americanese. "Look, man, you cats got a deal and don't know it. If you don't know what you're doing here, maybe nobody else does. Why don't you take off them goddamned flimsy rags, put on your fatigues and go on over to the Provost Marshall and ask him for transportation. He don't know where you're from and he don't what you're doing here. According to them tags, you're a Lieutenant. Shit, man. You're entitled to transportation."

The tags did say BOWERS, J.B. LIEUTENANT, and some numbers and Hank's tags said he was a Lieutenant, too. Damn right. We had both been commissioned Second Lieutenants in the Liberian Militia last year at home. Maybe that's how we got on the plane in the first place. Now, things weren't all that crazy. They began to make sense. The big, black PFC had told us that his name was Al Norfleet. "Come over here. See that gate over there? Go right up to that MP and tell him you want transportation. He'll send you over to the motor pool and they'll give you a jeep.'" "Motor pool? What the hell is a motor pool?" "Man, that's where they keep all the rolling stock. Where the hell you guys from, again?" "Li-be-ri-a." "Okay. You just do what I tell you. He'll give you a jeep. When you get it, I'll be standing right over here. You do know how to drive, don't you?"

We did as we had been told, and sure enough, we got a jeep. We never even had to see the Provost Marshall. Al had followed us at a safe distance taking no chances on these two hicks. He had offered to drive the jeep. We drove past a gasoline pump, parked, and said nothing. The soldier at the station filled the tank without a word and off we drove into the dark. Al said it was a few miles into town. Downtown was the Victoria Hotel. There was always a ball down there. The broads were nice. Very obliging. "You don't need any money, man. You got transportation. That's the shit, man. These are the cats off the post. They'll buy the drinks. I'll tell them your story. You don't need to say nothing. You got transportation, and they can ride back with you. They won't have to catch that bus at midnight.

Look man if the chicks don't act right, talk some of that African language. Say anything African. They won't know what the hell's going on. Show them those gold chains. You can even give 'em one of the chains if they don't come through otherwise. Hell, all you got to do is steal it back from under the pillow when you leave. That's just where she'll put it. Anything you give them, they'll reach right up and put it under the pillow. That's where they put money when they get paid. You might even come out a few bucks ahead. You can steal your chain back and the loot she got from the guy before you. Can't never tell, man. You in business now."

With an expert tutor like Al and a little bit of imagination and cunning, we were accomplished flim-flam artists within a week. By the second week, we were masters at the trading of tickets for a joint or two from the local street urchins that always hung around the army base. The little Brazilian boys didn't know the difference. They called us Joe, too, just like they called the GIs. Everybody on the post could tell we weren't American, but how were these local kids to know the difference? We were just two black GIs. They couldn't differentiate that Geschee accent that gave us away whenever we tried to pass as real GIs.

After two full weeks, we were still in Brazil. One morning we got up and Al was gone. The other fellows said he had left on a flight the night before. Reality set in again. How were we ever getting out of here? No one on the base had any advice for us. We decided to go looking for the American Consul. Downtown was the American Consulate. We walked in wearing our fatigue uniforms. When we told our story, the consular official was visibly incredulous. "Niggers think they're smart. Always want to start some shit," he must have thought. He asked, "Where did you say you came from? How long have you been here?" Then after mulling it over, "Well, I'll see what can be done, but we have no responsibility for you, you know. I suspect you should have been on one of the Pan American flights a day or two after you got here. Anyway, we'll see. You say you're going to school? Well, most schools in the United States started two weeks ago, son."

At this point, Hanks stood there, tears streaming down his face. The American Consul made several telephone calls from one or the other of the two phones that seemed to have a thousand buttons that flashed on and off, whether the phone rang or not. Finally, he said,

"Okay. You boys might be able to get on a flight tomorrow morning. It's a charter with some tobacco men from the States and there are a couple of vacant seats. Be here at 7:30 a.m. and I'll show you where to go."

We were at the office by 6:30 a.m. the following morning, sitting on the steps with two battered cardboard suitcases, waiting. The janitors came and looked and passed on. Finally, the Consul showed up and we went in. He talked on the telephone again. This time, it seemed as though he was pleading with somebody on the other end. He reminded them of the previous day's promise. Then, there was relief. "Okay, okay. Thanks a lot Jim," he had said. "Come on, you boys. And when you get on, you'd better stay put until you're in Miami."

So, we got on the chartered flight and took off. While visions of what it must be like in America punctuated our daydreams, the large man across the isle had noticed the fine leather boots on my feet and inquired where I had gotten them. That was a patent invitation to a deal on the spot. "Want to buy them?" I asked. The man said yes and soon the deal was closed at twenty-five bucks. Off with the boots. Into the cardboard suitcase and back on with the old ox hide shoes I had left home with. Well, the old shoes weren't all that bad and besides, they went better with the old, flimsy blue suit I had on, anyway. The sharp Brazilian boots had been sort of contradictory. In any case, it was clear profit because I hadn't bought the boots. A local vendor had paid his fare from downtown to the Army base with those boots.

The plane hopped up and down at all the routine stops, almost hourly it seemed. The names sounded like a tourist travelogue. "Forteleza, San Luaza, Belem." Belem was an overnight stop and a magnificent chance to gamble. Right there in the airport was a big jackpot. You could buy a chance on a bet that it wouldn't rain that day. For something like a quarter or fifty cents, one stood a chance of winning several thousands of dollars. Incredible. Especially when you looked up at the bright blue sky. "These folks have got to be crazy," I thought. I took five dollars worth of tickets and began to prepare a shopping list in my mind. Brown shoes, black shoes, white and brown, white and black. Oh I was a nut about shoes! I just had to wait until six that evening, the hour for collecting, because I'd have made it then. I figured, "I've got these bastards beat at their own game." How the hell did I know that it had rained every day for umpteen years in this town perched right on top of the equator? Hell, I was no meteorologist, and I didn't ask any questions. Most tourists bought one ticket each. That should have given us a clue, but maybe they didn't need the money. The way I figured it, it would take at least a five dollar investment to assure enough winnings to take care of my shopping list.

Well, that beautiful bubble burst when at 5:30 p.m. sharp, out of nowhere, the heavens opened and it rained like hell for just about five minutes and promptly stopped. I'll be damned. Just liked a day in July in Monrovia. Maybe the people who set the odds knew something. Of course they did. And in a way, they had provided this guinea fowl with his first memorable lesson on the percentages in gambling. The people who make the odds are always the smart ones. Those who play the game are the suckers. That thought has stuck indelibly over the years.

Back on the plane the next day, we continued the hop to the United States. The next stop for the night was Port of Spain, Trinidad. This was the land of Rum and Coca Cola, just like the song said. First order of the day was to look for Point Koomana! Was that a real place or just some words in a song? The taxi driver assured us it was indeed a real place and offered to take us there. This was just the beginning of my long association with, and study of, the behavior of taxi drivers, worldwide. They always seem to know the score and they always seem to reflect the mood of the community in which they work. In almost thirty years, and from Rome to Hong Kong to Dakar the story is always the same; the fast-talking, smart-ass cabbie in New York City is as much a barometer of the metropolitan jungle as the smooth, man-about-town cabbie at Disneyland who happens to be a connoisseur of Hollywood and a pal of the movie stars. Similarly, the lunatic race car driver who passes for a cabbie in Rome and who, conveniently, miscounts and shortchanges you, is fair warning of what you can expect in that Eternal City. And so is the taxi driver in Alicante, Spain who will drive all night for two small boys, looking for the relatives who were supposed to meet them, even turning off the meter at 800 pesetas when he realizes they are lost. Each cab driver is a reflection of the morals and mores of his society.

But at Point Koomana in 1946, Hank and I negotiated a jug of local Rum and a bottle of Coca Cola syrup. There were no pre-mixed bottles in those days. You got Coca Cola syrup in a glass bottle and mixed it up yourself, and it tasted even better then than it does today. We set out for the beach. It was no sweat finding company. Two chicks that came over to inspect us, just like their blood sisters in Brazil, were immediately fascinated by the shiny gold chains Hank wore. Repeat performance. "Is that real gold?" "Yep." "Where are you from?" "Liberia."   By this time, we knew the advantage of our newfound status, so without further question we informed our hostesses that we were GIs returning to the U.S. from some mission. Just what mission, we didn't say. But any sort of vague identification with the U.S. and a GI status meant greenbacks, and that meant that you had money to spend, wouldn't be there for long, and you didn't have the time or patience to beg for it. You were ready to pay for it. How much? That was another question, but these girls were obviously professionals, and no doubt they were accomplished in the barter system. "After all, those gold chains must be dirt cheap in Africa. These two hicks could be 'taken' very easily," they must have thought. They had no way of knowing we had been tutored in the art of reaching under the pillow. So, without too much talk, the deal was closed. They would lie there on the beach and drink with us, then go into town, perhaps to a dance hall, and then finally, we would shack up with them for the night, if the price were right.

At nightfall, we took off for town. "Let's go home," Hank had suggested. "No, no, no. First, get something to eat," and then there was a grand dance being held at some place or other. One of the girls had said that her brother played in the band there. Later that night when the fight broke out, it turned out that the guy in the band said she was his wife, not his sister, and he charged Hank with "alienation of affections" and proceeded to reach for the gold chains around Hank's neck.

The fight had actually been started somewhere else in the dance hall. We didn't know who was fighting whom, or why, but it must have presented a good opportunity for the con man in the band to pull a fast one, and perhaps share the loot with our hostesses. We had seen through the "sister" long ago, when as soon as we arrived at the dance hall, she had "gone to the restroom" and stayed for almost an hour. Hank had taken off the chains and secured them in a little bag around his waist. This little waist purse is what the Krio people in Sierra

Leone call a Kotoku. So, when the drummer reached out and found no chains, we faked him out of position by assuring him that his "sister" must have already taken the chains. When she couldn't convince her brother/husband/accomplice or whatever he was to the contrary, their little game was over. Amidst their accusations, we pretended to search frantically for the gold chains. The husband/brother/drummer gave up in disgust just before the police raided the place. Hank and I were too busy escaping for the adultery charges to be pressed. The girls, for their part, stayed on our tails. After escaping the melee, we re-grouped across the street. With considerable flourish and bravado, we threatened to pistol-whip the girls if they didn't admit to their scam. They promptly confessed.

At this point any sensible man would have quit and gone back to the hotel. But at eighteen, intoxicated by our newly acquired freedom, we did the natural thing. We went home with the girls. After all, they were the principal commodities we had come after; the dance hall had only been an interlude. The little shack among the hovels of Lacoule Street was hardly fit to be called a bordello. It was a single room covered with tin and a flimsy curtain separated the two beds. Hank and his girl got the real bed. The cot in the corner was left to my mate and me. It was sometime near dawn when we discovered that this was an auntie and niece affair. Hank had the auntie. Of course, an argument ensued when she had attempted to charge him double. Hank had insisted that the price he had already negotiated was for everything that happened – all night. Auntie had a more conservative definition. She apparently was charging per orgasm. Well, by that count, I should have paid nothing! While my girl went through a very elaborate cleansing procedure, insisting that she wanted to make sure that her moneymaker didn't get polluted, I had spilled all of my business somewhere between the hard mattress and her thighs. She swore it had been in the right place; I swore it had not and demanded a replay. She demanded a double fee. I protested. In sheer fatigue and, perhaps, shame, I had fallen asleep. With Hank's very vocal protest and Auntie's counter threat of mayhem to us both, I was suddenly wide-awake. Hank and I won the argument, if one could call that a win. We paid five bucks each and departed for the hotel amidst loud protests.

Having no idea of directions, it was some time before we found a taxi back to the Hotel de France.

Back at the hotel, we were met by a stern Englishman who demanded to know where we had been all night. He said that seeing as how we were minors, he had been responsible for us and had been looking for us all night. Anyway, the guests on the charter flight had already left the hotel and the plane was due to be taking off just about now, he said. Our insolence didn't help any. Hank told the Englishman to go to hell and I found myself muttering something to the effect that the gentleman should go screw himself. We packed up and rushed out, nonetheless, making it aboard the plane just before the doors closed.

The flight to Port of Prince, Haiti and then to San Juan, Puerto Rico went by between naps. The kind of naps one takes per force due to a hangover. And this was a hangover of major proportions. The only things I remembered were like instant replays of first impressions.

Once we landed in San Juan, though, there was too much excitement to sleep. Everything was new. Buildings were all so big and everywhere there were so many people. People going, people coming, not seeming to know each other or care where each other went. The instant impression I got at the airport in San Juan was that there seemed to be so much food – snacks, meals, drinks, everything — and there seemed to be so many toilets. This toilet business was apparently big business here. There were even a few booths that were coin operated. My curiosity got the best of me at one of these pay toilets in the San Juan Airport, and so I dropped a nickel into the slot to investigate the facilities. What was the difference between this one and the outside one you could use for free? I didn't detect a difference.

Later on in the United States during my first weeks, I continued this bizarre line of research. Everywhere that people transacted business of any sort, it seemed, there was a snack bar and a toilet. That was reasonable upon reflection. After all, if one ate or drank constantly, one should have the means of disposing of the ultimate metabolic end products. That made sense. But why were some toilets free and some coin operated? I have never been able to answer that one satisfactorily, even after living for so long in the United States. Perhaps it has something to do with supply and demand. Or perhaps there are some people who are so status-oriented that they would never take anything for free. The reasoning seems to be that it must be inferior if it is free. In fact, after years of living in America, as a medical student in major metropolitan hospitals, I came to confirm this impression of the American way. It is stigmatizing to get anything free. For example, there was the old bum at Kansas City General Hospital who protested, "I ain't no goddamned charity case. I pay my way." When the admissions clerk had added up the charges and given him the bill, he protested again that she was cheating. After almost an hour of investigation into his family size, rate of wages and an explanation of the sliding scale of charges, he protested and insisted on paying the higher rate, even though it meant owing the city.

These were all very valuable lessons in human nature and in the study of social systems. Even today, I sometimes wonder what they mean, and I am still not sure that I understand all their implications. It seems that the stigma is not so much in getting something for free. It is the appearance of being a public charge. In fact, there is merit in getting stuff free, provided you're slick enough to beat the system. There is merit in beating the system, whether it is the government, a mail-order house or a radio talk show. As long as you are not branded a welfare recipient, there is merit in getting anything that you can for free.

On that fateful flight into Miami in 1946, the plane landed at about 8 p.m. It was late September or early October so it was already dark. Rolling along from the point of touchdown to the terminal seemed halfway across the world. The airline hostess had indeed said that this was Miami when we landed. Could they have forgotten to completely stop and let us off? Had they been mistaken and would they take off again? I knew one thing for sure. Whenever in doubt, keep your damned mouth shut and watch what other people do. So I asked no questions. And since everybody else seemed relaxed, except for Hank, I thought it must be okay. It was always reassuring to look at Hank because, compared to him, I was so self-assured. Since he was even greener than me, if I showed any doubt, Hank would surely panic. "You think we're still in Miami?" he asked in a hoarse whisper after we had been taxiing for some time. "Sure, man. Can't you see how relaxed all these people are? They're going to Miami, too," I said soothingly wondering if what I said was true.

Finally, the plane stopped, the door opened and a man came aboard and sprayed the entire cabin with a suffocating chemical. It smelled like a mixture of the same stuff that the American Army used to spray mud puddles back in Monrovia. "What the hell is that for?" Hank whispered. "I guess they know where we're from," I replied. "It must be DDT."

Going through Customs at Miami was my first encounter with America the beautiful. To anyone not knowing the many things about America and Americans that one learns from living among them, this would be a terrifying experience. The Customs man had asked in his natural tone of voice, "Do you have anything to declare?" To me, that was a loaded question. Could this guy have known that I had stolen my father's pearl-handled 22-caliber pistol and stashed it in my suitcase? Was this a routine question? What did he mean by "anything to declare?" The thought of being deported even before being admitted; the thoughts of shattering my dream of becoming a doctor and of going to prison, terrified me. Good God! Why did I do it? What would I do with a pistol in America, anyway? My mind was racing. Shaking like a leaf and sweating a cold sweat had given me away.

The Customs officer didn't need a degree in criminology to detect that something was wrong. I fumbled with my suitcase, opened it, and immediately lifted up a few pieces of clothing, exposing the gun. The Customs officer simply looked at it, took it, and handed it to a colleague standing by and they both seemed amused for some reason. The next question bore no relationship to the crisis at hand. "How much do you weigh?" he asked. "One hundred twenty-five pounds," came my stuttering answer. Both men laughed loudly, looking at each other. "How much you say you weigh?" "One twenty-five," I answered, this time with a faint trace of anger and embarrassment. When the officer recovered his composure, he cracked, "maybe that's what you weighed when you left home, but hell, you ain't one ounce over ninety pounds, soaking wet. Ha. Ha. Ha." He laughed again, showing my passport to several men milling around, who also laughed like hell. Nobody ever said anything about the gun. I had unloaded it before packing it in the suitcase. The five shells were still in my pocket, but no one asked any questions. They didn't search me, and, of course, I said nothing else. The officer eventually pointed the way and Hank and I moved on through the line. I had not figured out what was so funny.

After getting on the bus for Atlanta, I pulled out my passport and looked at the picture. A childhood pal who dabbled in photography had taken it. In those days there were no passport photo studios in Monrovia. One did the best one could. This was my best, but truthfully, it was a funny picture. I looked at it, and suddenly I realized how comical it was. I began to laugh. I was only mildly distressed when that passport got lost in the mail two years later and had to be replaced by the Liberian Embassy in Washington. It was, in fact, a relief. My new passport showed me togged down in one of my best $19.95 suits from Stein Brothers, hair slicked back with Murray's pomade, and all the accouterments that any self-respecting black dude affected in those days. I was "as sharp as a mosquito's peter," as the boys in Atlanta would say.

The decision to take a bus to Atlanta had been elementary. The Bishop of the Methodist church back home had recommended that we get the first thing moving out of Miami. "Don't stay in Miami any longer than you have to," he had told us. There was no question of flying. We couldn't afford it. The next train was scheduled to leave four hours later at 2:00 a.m. and the train station was across town. A nice black man, wearing a red cap, told us there was a bus for Atlanta every hour on the hour. He told us to get on the Airport Bus and tell the driver that we wanted to go to the bus terminal. The instructions were very explicit. Moreover, they were simple to follow. How the hell could we have known the difference between going by bus and going by train? Anyway, we would soon be in Atlanta, I thought.

Not being able to imagine any road so long that a bus could run for twenty-four hours on it and still be going somewhere is truly a state of innocence. Hank and I started looking for signs that would say Atlanta about two hours out of Miami. When the bus changed drivers, we were positive that the new driver could not know that we were going to Atlanta, so we went up and tried to tell him. One snarl from him and we went back to the back of the bus and proceeded to sob quietly. Why had we ever come to this place? Why the hell do we have to sit in the back, when there were so many empty seats up front, and that's where we wanted to sit? There were a lot of vacant seats in the middle, too. Why did we have to sit in the back by this frowsy, drunken old man who got on bus after us? He obviously smelled and nobody in his right mind would want to sit next to him. Our questions would be answered within the next twenty-four hours.

There was the first rest stop. We had followed the line of passengers into the restaurant and stood there waiting for our orders to be taken. As anybody in America in 1946 could have told us, nothing happened. We had not noticed that everybody else from the back of the bus had disappeared to somewhere else. When it was time to board again, we got back on, hungry, figuring that the stop hadn't been long enough, so we'd wait for the next stop.

At the next stop there was nobody else in the back of the bus, so we missed the point again. Same result as before. Two stops later there was still nobody else in the back of the bus, but things were faintly desperate. Thirst was the main problem this time. Never mind the food, just let us get a little water to drink. By this time we had suspected that maybe we weren't being served because we were black. But it was only a suspicion. Maybe they just don't serve black people. Maybe they just don't like black people. Okay. Well, we'll just get a drink of water and wait until we get to Atlanta. As we walked over to the water fountain, a fat man weighing at least 300 pounds and wearing a chef's high hat, came over and scowled. "Git away from that, boy." Still innocent, we sauntered over to the counter, placed a quarter down and said in unison, "Coca Cola." For some reason, the counter girl served us two Coca Colas. The same fat man rushed over, snatched the paper cups from us and dumped them into the trash shoving us out of the door and throwing the quarter behind us. We got the message, then.

Old sage that I was, I reckoned, "Hank, this must be what they call Jim Crow." "You know what? That must be why those other black people disappeared some place else," Hank said. "Maybe that's why they told us to sit back here. Maybe that's why this bus driver, who was smiling and cheerful, suddenly got mad when we asked him how far it was to Atlanta. Maybe we're lucky that fat man didn't stab or shoot us. Maybe we'd better just stay on this damned bus until we see somebody black and ask them what is going on." Soon a black man did get on, and he confirmed our worst suspicions, but he said it wouldn't have made any difference if we had come by train. There would have been a separate car for blacks. The only difference is that this car would have been up front, right behind the engine. Why was this reversed when it was a train? He said he didn't rightly know why, but that was the way it was. He was surprised that we didn't know about this. In any case, at the next stop the black man got off and brought back two cokes for us. We offered to pay him, but he said no, no, no, that was okay. As he left the bus about an hour before the Atlanta stop, he looked back at us sorrowfully. Hank broke down and wept like a baby. He was still weeping loudly as I left the bus in Atlanta. He had to continue even farther into the hinterland of America.

The one big difference I noted once I got to Atlanta was that there were many black people moving around and not seeming to pay any attention to the white people. The red caps were all black, of course, but there were also some other black people who seemed to feel free. They didn't seem to stop and bow and scrape to the big-bellied white men that seemed to be standing in uniform at every stop we had made before Atlanta. It was impossible to be sure whether these uniformed men were policemen or bus drivers or cab drivers. For the first twenty-four hours that I was in America, all big-bellied white men in uniform looked the same to me. They all seemed heavily armed. They all appeared pleasant and courteous from a distance, but they all got mad whenever you approached them. Maybe it was because of the way I was dressed. Or maybe, I concluded, this was a reflex reaction. Big-bellied white men in uniform got mad when they saw black people; that was all. Perhaps they were paid to be mean to black people and to destroy them upon the slightest provocation. Who knew? Maybe they could kill you any time they wanted. Maybe there would be no penalty. This very elementary thesis, as crude as it sounds, was the essence of my orientation to American society, and even after fifteen years of living in America, climbing the social ladder from bus boy to resident surgeon in some of the finest hospitals in America, I never found any convincing proof that the contrary was really true. The absolute tragedy of it all was that I found this theory to be the precise feeling of much of the lower class in America—black and white. If you were poor, a white man in a uniform was your enemy. So, the game of life in America could be simplified. The solution: get out of the lower class!

Actually, in retrospect, my first twenty-four hours in America were very soundly educational. But education is not always absorbed, especially if one is not conditioned. So, within two months of my arrival in Atlanta, I almost made an error in judgment. It was in the fall, perhaps November or early December, but it was still warm enough in Atlanta to go without a topcoat, especially if you didn't own one. My roommate and I had gone downtown one Saturday morning, shopping. For me, it would be mostly window-shopping. I had no money. I went for the experience. The only thing I needed or could afford to buy would be an extra reed for the old clarinet I had brought with me to amuse myself. I had visions of trying out for the college band. An extra reed would cost about fifty cents. I could handle that.

As we strolled along Spring Street, I noted a store window in which there were some musical instruments. There were also lots of other things. Most memorable for me, however, was the clearly marked designation, WHITES ONLY.

Chicago

As long as I remained safely in the community of the black college elite in the South, life in America was spirited but without exceptional challenges. It was during those summer holidays working in the "Windy City" that I would gain new insights into the American way.

"Chicago, Chicago, that Toddlin' Town

Chicago, Chicago, I'll show you around

I love it…

Bet your bottom dollar you'll lose

The blues

In Chicago,

Chicago, Chicago…the folks who

Visit…

All want to settle down."

Fred Fisher, 1922

That popular song from the Roaring Twenties could be taken literally in that era, and perhaps for a generation after, when the massive tide of black migration from the South was in full swing. Sharecroppers and farm hands from Georgia and Mississippi mingled easily with the "street dudes." Which was a good thing, at least from one point of view. It made the bumpkins from the bayous proud of themselves for the first time... at being "citified." From the viewpoint of the artful city slickers, this sudden influx worked both ways – sometimes good, because their con games were more easily executed upon these hapless strangers; or bad, because the big, bad Polish cops who walked the streets of Chicago whipped heads with impunity in the name of controlling the ominous rise of street crime that was heralded by this wave of human beings migrating northward. Without a doubt, some of this may have been justified, but to those of us who were closer to the potential receiving end of a nightstick, it always seemed excessive and undue force. For me, this was only a reinforcement of the initial negative impression I had gathered regarding American law enforcement personnel. Even after almost forty years, I can't truthfully say that this feeling has been erased to any significant degree.

The end of World War II only intensified the migration north. No young Negro in his right mind was about to go back to Ruleville, Mississippi after discharge from Service, when he could stop in Chicago, get a job and hang out on the South Side in style. Man, there was something for everybody. If you were ambitious you could work the midnight shift at the stockyards, go to college on the GI Bill, and still have all the time in the world to raise hell half the night on South Park or 63rd Street. You could catch every big band that came to town – somewhere. If not downtown, then when they made the scene at the Regal on 47th Street, or when they dropped in after hours at the Club DeLisa on State Street and Garfield Boulevard. Those were the days. Those were the late forties. I knew a fellow who worked on the lathe next to me at the leather goods factory on the North Side, who in a single weekend, got to see – live in Chicago, Illinois Jacquet, Lester Young, Ella Fitzgerald and Billy Eckstine – all the greatest in one weekend – and he still had time to hang around the local club on 63rd Street where Gene Ammons and his group held forth when they weren't on the road. It was like heaven – if that was what you enjoyed.

For me, all of that would have been wonderful, if I didn't have to work so damned hard to make it. Whenever I think of Chicago, Club DeLisa, the Regal Theater and Joe's Place, I always think of the two hour ride every morning, taking first one bus, then the EL and finally another bus, just to get to the factory. After nine hours, repeating the whole trip in reverse. When you left home it was dark, and when you got home it was damned near dark again, even in the summertime.

It seemed that every job was a backbreaking enterprise. First there was the job at the sandblasting plant, which consisted of driving a truck backward and forward all of fifty feet all day. You used a crane attached to the truck to lift these old cars and ferry them into the sandblasting pit and out again. Even for something this simple, the monotony was devastating. Fortunately or unfortunately, I didn't last very long on that job. A boom, carelessly swung in my direction with the switch turned on by a co-worker who had become peeved for some now forgotten but trivial reason, landed squarely against my cheek, flattening one side of my face for nearly six months. At the same time, this succeeded in disclosing my illegal employment status, thereby disqualifying me for compensation. In a single act of petty meanness, a near tragedy had occurred. I shall never forget the proprietor of that little plant. He had knowingly hired me without proper documentation and without even a Social Security number. He did it because I told him I was seeking summer employment in order to get back into school in the fall. When the "accident" happened, he actually had no obligation to me, certainly no legal obligation. He knew that very well. But he explained that reporting the accident would expose his illegal activity. He directed me to a clinic where I could receive treatment at a nominal fee, and he kept me on his payroll for the rest of the summer, at what were substantial wages for that time. He and every one else at the plant had been convinced that the injury had been intentionally perpetrated, and the fellow who did it had been fired at the same time that I was laid off.

Through all of this, the greatest impression made upon me was the very casual offer of a friend of the relatives I was living with at the time. He wanted me to give him the name of the co-worker who had caused the injury and a general idea of the section of town he lived in. He said he would trace this fellow and somehow, I don't know how, get a picture taken of him to show to me for positive identification.

Once I identified my assailant positively, Charlie promised he would have him killed! Just like that. Since he was a friend of my relatives, Charlie said he wouldn't even require his customary fee of $200 or $300. He would do it for free! I was terrified at this casual offer of help, and he must have sensed my fear because Charlie smiled and said, "We won't involve you at all, you just point him out and we'll take care of it and you don't need to know anything about it." This was my first encounter with the sordid business of hit men. My relatives assured me that Charlie meant it. They had positive evidence that this was one of his sidelines. Of course, he had a regular job too. He was a diesel mechanic somewhere. His boss was a character who was in the business of changing the identity of automobiles and selling them. In other words, they ran a car-stealing ring. Charlie was a killer for hire on the side.

After the sandblast job, I worked at the leather goods factory on the North Side. This factory was so far north in Chicago that my relatives frequently joked that I worked in "Milwaukee."

Perhaps it was the monotony of traveling back and forth to mind-numbing jobs that made my buddies and me do the silly things we did. Perhaps it was to relieve the boredom. Like the days we would walk into the EL station, read the signs that said, "Do not walk on the tracks" or "Danger. Do not walk beyond this point," and then walk calmly by onto the tracks. The idea was to hop onto the train as it slowed around the curve, thereby avoiding the purchase of a fifteen-cent ticket. But since you had no ticket, you also had no transfer to get on the bus – the second leg of the trip. To solve that little problem, you simply waited until your stop came up, and you walked past the lady at the exit door and simply snatched a transfer and kept moving. If there were four or five of you, she knew better than to protest. So that is how you got home at a grand savings of fifteen cents! I don't know about the other kids who played this game when I did, but for me, the fear of what would happen if I were ever challenged was the thrill. As it happened, I was never challenged. In years to come, I always felt a sort of kinship with those troubled youngsters who did not get away and who were eventually labeled as juvenile delinquents. In retrospect, it all seems so pointless that to save fifteen cents one would place himself at risk by violating three or four city ordinances, and even risk loss of life or a limb. These are the perils of youth. Given a few changes of circumstances, a bit more instability at home, or, perhaps, less motivation, an innocent prankster could become the city's next felon. I am sure many youngsters who wound up in prison began in just this way.

For my part, there was always the end of summer. And there was never the thought of dropping out of school. For one thing, after working at any one of these menial jobs for three months, there was enough motivation to return to college.

What is definitely true is the fact that continuous exposure to violence has the effect of raising one's tolerance for violence. Some of my relatives would have been shocked by some of my encounters at work. For others, it would have been familiar. In fact, I picked up a few lessons in what I call "satisfactory handling of evidence," from one of these relatives. The occasion was a payday Friday. One of those days when we indulged in the routine of walking on the train tracks at the station. Only, on paydays, a part of the sequence consisted of first cashing the paycheck and buying a half-pint of Yellowstone bourbon whiskey at the nearby liquor store. Upon breaking the seal, you took a swig out of the flask and proceeded with the routine of walking past the ticket counter and on to the train tracks.

On this particular Friday the routine of stealing a transfer moved along without a hitch. Even the third and final leg of my return home by catching the South Parkway bus went without a hitch. It was just about dusk as I got off the bus and proceeded to cross the street. Suddenly, I was tackled from behind by a youth who was about my size. He was an expert because he knew exactly where to reach. Most dudes carried their money in their shirt pocket located over the left breast. He reached in, snatched the envelope and proceeded to move. Any sensible person would have simply let it go. But at age nineteen or twenty, impulses don't flow that way. I gave him the chase he deserved. Upon catching him, I wasn't surprised to discover that he had a switchblade. Not being of that breed myself, I did not have my blade with me. Of course I owned one and carried it most of the time, but, inevitably, on this day of all days, I was unarmed. After a brief but violent struggle, I managed to retrieve my pay envelope and my assailant's switchblade. The rules of the game called for inflicting enough injury to assure your attacker's incapacity. I proceeded to carry this out with cool efficiency although I had no intention of mortal injury. I have not the slightest ideas how many wounds I inflicted upon this chap, but they were multiple, and in later years I often tried to imagine what his face and neck looked like once he was repaired. In my inexperience, I was sufficiently frightened to go back to the park the next day searching for his body in case I had unintentionally killed him. Apparently, I had not. At least he wasn't lying there. But, from the looks of my shirt when I left the scene the night before, you could not have proved I hadn't killed someone.

As I fled the scene, I had approached a cop on the beat. I got the standard response. The conversation went like this:

"Hey Cop, I've just been attacked. I was robbed. There's the fellow over there. I got him back, but he's lying over there." Drawing his pistol the cop said, "Step back, man. Fall back. Get away. If you want to file a complaint, I have to take you down to the station. If you don't want to file a complaint, I didn't see you, man, get the hell away, man."

He was a big, black cop, but he appeared at least as afraid of me as I had been of my assailant. I dashed into the house after being careful to run at least five doors past my place, to be sure I had misled the policeman, and then doubled back through the alley and up the back stairway. Somewhere along the way, I had been told how to evade the police by running past your door, then doubling back. I can't remember who told me, but it made sense to me. As I entered the apartment, my cousin, Roy, must have recreated the scene I had fled in his mind. Without asking any questions, he instructed me in the proper handling of evidence. This consisted of stuffing all blood stained clothing into the commode, and taking a swift cold shower immediately. By the time I was out of the shower, Roy had returned from the corner store with a large can of caustic soda, which he applied to the commode rendering my shirt no more than liquefied pulp that flushed easily through the system. The fact that there was no door to door search by the cops later that night was considered further evidence that my counter-attack had been less than fatal.

Chicago meant all of these things to me. Fortunately, with the passage of time, the tough grind of the factories receded to the depths of remote memory, leaving mostly the remembrances of good times – like the New Year's Eve at the DeLisa, the first time ever that I was drunk off of champagne. A pure champagne high. The real stuff, bubbly French champagne, consumed ice cold in huge gulps that were enough to fill you before making your really drunk. Not just in little sips like you get at ceremonial receptions. A high off of that much champagne, one never forgets. Even much better champagne, served aboard a yacht anchored offshore in the Greek Isles, complete with the best Iranian caviar, could not compare with that first champagne high.

By the time I got to know somebody who had a yacht anchored off the Greek Isles, I was old enough to have been around. I had done so much that the comparisons tended to blur. But that first high, I can never forget. Its like the first time ever sleeping out away from home, in somebody else's bed; where her folks didn't know you were in the house and might have killed her if they had known she would do such a thing. Even your own folks would stay up worrying about you and thinking you had lost the way home or taken the wrong bus in the big city. They would never dream where you actually were.

My relatives in Chicago had made their views as clear as Gina's folks had. "At nineteen, you're both too young," Aunt Mandy had said. "And besides that, with all the nice girls of our own, why do you have to have a white girlfriend? Her people will never accept you." Gina's father, a policeman, had already told her what he would do to her if she ever went out with a black man. He wasn't prejudiced, he had told her. He just believed in the purity of both races. So we both knew that anything we did was forbidden. Both by her family and mine. So we had limited our affair to necking in the movie matinees on our days off and to minor erotic experiments in heavy petting in her car on the edge of the park. It was too risky to drive all the way inside of the park. One never knew when one would be taken in by the cops or attacked by a street character looking for a victim. A bit of experience had proven for us that you were much less likely to be investigated by the cops if you did whatever you did right on the edge of the park. It seems that the cops never figured anyone would be so bold.

The first time we tried it, it worked beautifully. In fact, it worked so well that we established a routine of just stopping on the edge of the park or practically in the street and just doing everything we wanted to do right out there. The cops would pass by, going into the park to look for hidden offenders. Eventually we decided that it was too inconvenient to be out there screwing in the streets. Why not go home? As for me, I could not risk taking her to my place. My aunt was one of those people who suffered chronic insomnia. I am not sure if she ever slept more than four hours any night unless she was ill. So that was out of the question. Besides, Aunt Mandy was so righteous and upstanding; I had every reason to believe that she would have turned me in to the police herself if I brought that girl into her house. Gina's father, the policeman, just knew that nobody would be so bold as to creep into his house. And his little girl would be the last to ever bring anyone into his house. So, we figured her place, the most unlikely accommodation, was, ironically, the safest. It became our regular rendezvous spot.

Of all the beautiful memories of Chicago, the most poignant for me, was the memory of that passionate love affair. We were two teenagers from two very different worlds. And we were passionate in our lovemaking. Our affair lasted for five years although we were only together during the summers and Christmas holidays when I came to Chicago to work. She was bold enough or crazy enough or innocent enough to offer to come to Atlanta where I was in school to be with me. She said she would run away and not care what her parents said or thought. But, I had lost my innocence and become so conditioned by the realities of day-to-day separatism that was America. I discouraged any such rash moves. By the time Gina had worked halfway through her masters degree in clinical psychology and I had started medical school, we both had a firmer intellectual basis for appreciating the futility of continuing our relationship. She swore that we would be lovers forever, and that I could only nullify that promise by failing to keep in touch regardless of whether she ever married. For my part, I could only swear that I would never forget. Visions of the trauma that our union would have inflicted on both our families and ourselves were enough to deter me even if it was true love.

Gina and I had no ordinary thing. During the first summer we spent together when we barely knew each other, Gina had remembered the address of the tenement house where I lived deep in the South Side Ghetto.

On a fateful July morning, as I lay sleeping, having returned only two hours earlier from my five to midnight waiter's job downtown, a fire had broken out. It was one of those fires that periodically consumed entire neighborhoods in this particular section of Chicago. As it turned out, I was the last to escape the inferno. And, it turned out that this was due mainly to Gina's efforts. She had remembered the address and when the early morning radio announcement was made that this block of Dearborn was burning, Gina had driven to the scene and pestered the firemen with her screams that she knew someone who was still in that house. She knew I would be in a deep sleep after a long night. I was actually awakened by the fireman's hacking at my bedroom window with an axe. I awoke and stumbled around intoxicated by fumes. I finally stumbled to the only remaining window not engulfed by flames and just jumped. The height was not more than ten feet. I shall never forget the extent of my possessions with which I had escaped. I had grabbed a suitcase containing the only suit I never wore – a tuxedo. I remember feeling very disgusted and unreasonably angry with the Red Cross worker who offered me a cup of coffee and a blanket. Why the hell would I need a blanket in the middle of July at 8:30 in the morning? And what good would the coffee do now that I was out there in my pajamas and mismatched shoes?

I sort of absently-mindedly walked away from the crowd, shrugging off the kind Red Cross lady who was urging the GI blanket along with a cup of coffee. Just then, I looked up and saw Gina standing on the edge of the crowd. I walked towards her self-consciously saying something like, "You know, I was only living here temporarily until my folks…" She embraced me before I could finish. Sobbing silently, she said, "Don't talk. Don't say anything. You don't need to explain. Just tell me where I can take you. I was so sure you were in there. I thought you hadn't made out. You know I can't take you home with me; I don't have money for a hotel. Where can I take you?" I thought about my chemistry professor at college with whom I had driven to Chicago for the summer. "Let's stop at that phone booth." At the phone booth, I made the call and, sure enough, he had heard of the fire too, but was uncertain of exactly where it was in relation to me. He had tried to call me but the lines had been down. We arranged that my professor would pick me up on the street corner and find temporary lodging for me over the weekend. The look on Gina's face as we drove away is one I'll never forget. As I think back on her quiet concern and on how we communicated, never having to say much to be understood, I realize that ours was a rare and special connection. "Don't talk. Don't say anymore. I understand. I know what you feel." Those were the feelings transmitted. And those were my most unforgettable memories of Chicago, Chicago – My Home Town.

The New Venture

Life in America improved for me as I climbed out of the low class status of immigrant student/menial laborer up the social ladder to permanent U.S. resident/medical doctor. I was still a Black man in a country obsessed with race and I did not yet earn a lot of money; but my potential and my education placed me in a position that was significantly more advantageous than it had been. I was one of only two Blacks placed as a surgical resident specializing in oncology at a prestigious New York City medical center.

I had married a beautiful, professional wife who was educated at the finest of American institutions of higher education and I was the proud father of two small children whose lives were pretty much guaranteed to be safely in the middle class. I had not begun to seriously consider returning home to Liberia. At least, I was not conscious of any real desire to go home. When one works as intensely for as many hours as medical interns and residents are required to, one has little time to ponder what will happen beyond being "on call" for the night. None-the-less, the thought of going home would soon begin to germinate and take root. My wife was a childhood friend from Liberia. She had taken for granted we would eventually return home to make our respective contributions, especially in view of the desperate need for professionals to develop our poor but proud native land. In the early '60s, we started to plan, in specific terms, our debut as young professionals on the Liberian scene.

One of the earliest discoveries I made upon returning to Africa as a General Surgeon and Oncology Specialist was that so many things needed to be done; it was just a matter of having the imagination to create a new service. Not that there was not enough to do at the Government Hospital. There was much more than any one man could handle. Being a government run institution, the frustration index was very high. It took ten days to get done any task for which you would estimate four hours. The red tape was formidable. At first, I lost myself in the work and refused to think about the bureaucracy, but that was stifling, to say the least.

In the meantime, whether I had intended to have a private practice of not, it was soon apparent that I would have to. The calls became more and more frequent – a virtual clamor! And then, there was the constant pressure to enter into contractual agreements – the businessmen, the Europeans, the diplomats, the international civil servants who wanted to know if my services could be had for a fee. If not on a daily basis, at least for an opinion, as a consultant. Would I agree to be a consultant to this Embassy or the other? Would I advise them when a case became too complicated for local management? Would I recommend repatriation and if so, what was the safest way to accomplish this?

This line questioning opened up a whole new horizon of possibilities. It was obvious that I needed a base of operations more satisfactory than anything available at the time. I needed, above all, a competent laboratory, and I needed it around the clock. People didn't plan accidents. If people knew when they would have heart attacks, they would conveniently arrange to have them in Europe or North America where there were coronary care units. So, as I reflect now, twenty years later, I realize that it was just as well that I knew so little about what was involved or required. If I had known more, I might have been too terrified to ever get started. But, I didn't know and I was young and ambitious. And, I loved my work. Sometimes I enjoyed it so much, I felt a little guilty for getting paid to have so much fun. Only in retrospect do I realize how much we were able to accomplish.

In order to fill this need, to be able to say when to evacuate, or when one might safely stay and wait, I began to develop a medical evacuation service. There was also an unspoken but strong sense of pride in being able to remove our country from the bottom of the list of places where it was truly perilous to become ill. It was bad enough to be among the poorest countries in the world. There was little I could do about that, but it seemed an unnecessary indignity to be among the most disadvantaged people on earth.

It didn't take long to get started on this formidable project, because, like myself, the other principal characters involved were young and innocent – but proud of their expertise in their respective areas. The architectural engineers were two of my friends who had also studied in the U.S. and returned home motivated to make a difference. They had never built a hospital or laboratory and I had never designed one either, though I had very definite ideas about what we needed. My wife, Lady, and I had cut out a picture of a building from a magazine when we were first married. I had said this would be my clinic, not having the vaguest notion of what one did inside a clinic. She had grinned and said that she would surround the place with flowers – bougainvillea and frangipanis of all hues. It would be beautiful. We would look at the picture, laugh and put it back into our scrapbook.

Now it was time to retrieve that model and deliver it to the architect. We got it and gave it to Barney. He didn't laugh. He was dead serious just as we had been. He showed it to his partner, Win, and they started designing and drawing and talking about soil analyses and structural steel strengths at various diameters. These sessions were mutually stimulating. I would tell them about the exciting medical challenges I faced and they would tell me about their entry into the various design competitions that came along in those days. They were even entering competitions for designing villas in the south of France and Spain as well as in other African countries. Lady seemed to know many things I had never considered. She knew just how wide windows were supposed to be, and Win always knew what shapes and contours suited our part of the world. Barney was just discarding his slide rule in favor of the calculator, which was coming into vogue at the time. They were not yet as small and thin and sophisticated as they would become, but they were a hell of a lot more refined than a slide rule.

Our sessions were solid work, but they were also relaxing and fun. After the workday, we would meet at their office or at mine and we would dream all of these outrageous dreams – with substantial help from a fifth of Jack Daniel's sour mash whiskey that we had all learned to appreciate in the U.S. South. We would dream about how we would extend our operations to cover at least the countries in the West African region – maybe even eventually having overseas extensions of our various enterprises. We would be as high as a kite for a couple of hours, but by the next day, we would have returned to the reality of the day-to-day grind of this sweet land of liberty – where the liberty itself was the only sweet thing. Every damned thing else was so hard to do that we often wondered if we had come back prematurely. But these recriminations were never long-lived. They were always transitory.

In the slow march of time we saw things happen. We saw the antiquated telephone system develop into a modern complicated system of microwaves and satellite signals. We saw running water improve to where it actually worked for more than twelve hours a day. We saw broad highways replacing ancient footpaths, and we saw what used to be two weeks of bone crushing walking in the bush country reduced to a three-hour drive. What was even better, we had been active in actually bringing about these changes.

We also saw the cost overruns by greedy contractors who cut corners leaving us with inundated telephone cables underground in a country where the yearly rainfall is over 200 inches, where the water table is just beneath the surface. We saw brand new roads spring potholes overnight, and we realized that it was much easier to call New York, London or Paris than it was to telephone each other locally. We lived daily with these dilemmas. From negotiating with other professionals – our counterparts from around the world – we learned the painful meaning of foreign aid. It was no consolation that we could hold our own with these European, American and Asian technocrats. Why shouldn't we have been able to do that? Always, lurking in one's consciousness was a feeling of guilt at being so far removed from the poor, suffering masses of humanity that was our country. But then, if we had not been far removed, how could we have built the buildings of which we were so proud? How could we have performed the surgical procedures that appeared to be miracles in Monrovia, and that *were* miracles when you considered the circumstances under which we operated? Many of the things we did would not have been considered routine anywhere. The fact of the matter is that almost nowhere, outside of the developing world, would the opportunity – the awesome responsibility of building a modern society – been thrust upon so few individuals.

From the first day that we opened, there was never a dull moment at the clinic. By the second year of our operations we had firmly established our presence locally and, to some extent, internationally. Our clinic had become known as a center for medical aid to sea-going vessels, and we unofficially collaborated with a network of advisors around the region extending from Southern Europe, via Gibraltar to Northern Africa and down the West Coast of Africa. A considerable number of Russian vessels in a fishing fleet that included crafts of all sizes formed a significant portion of the impromptu network of medical consultation cases. The quality of advice in those cases was, perhaps, not always optimum, and sometimes, it was less than certain that consultant and client understood each other. But, everything worked out in the balance. Many of the problems were not profound. When there were big problems, they were invariably overwhelming. Even in the trivial cases, I am sure it was reassuring to the anxious seamen that a doctor was listening.

Whenever we had a language barrier, it would be a triumphant moment when the breakthrough came in transmitting instructions. I was pleasantly surprised that we almost always found some common ground. Sometimes our conversations couldn't be recognized as an existing language. They would be a contrived blend of bits of Spanish, French, or Italian held together with simple English. And then, there were those reassuring words, "OKAY, OKAY." Everybody knew what that meant. This type of communication worked well except with the Greeks. Fortunately, there was usually someone around who could speak Greek and English. Once or twice, the translator turned out to be an official at the American Embassy. That was always amusing, since generally, the American community was the least likely source of linguists. Most meticulous were the Japanese, who always carried with them small phrase dictionaries. Some of the phrases were sidesplitting constructions, but, if we understood each other, that was all that mattered.

I could not have been happier. It seemed that in one move, I had satisfied all my yearnings, such as my love of ships and the sea; my love of languages and travel, and a life-long fascination with people of diverse cultures. Along with all this, there was the dramatic practice of medicine and the exhilarating feeling of doing something really worthwhile! As if this were not enough, I was even paid handsomely. Perhaps the best benefit was that, more than anything, it was educational. By this I mean education in the broadest sense of the term. Admittedly, when I think of some of the things I learned in my travels, I am straining the definition of "education." One such journey occurred in 1969.

It was a hot, humid night late in January when the call came crackling over the short wave radio at the port. There was a freighter on the high seas approximately four hours out of Monrovia and in distress because the Captain of the vessel had suddenly fainted and become disabled. The radio officer said he had a high fever and seemed to lapse into and out of consciousness. He further described the Captain as bleeding from the mouth and nose although not massively. Could they be accommodated at this port, or could we give them instructions for emergency care?

We judged that the history sounded too serious to tamper with instructions for long-term care. So we instructed them to come in, to be evaluated and receive advice. With an estimated time of arrival of four hours, we began to prepare for what we supposed the condition might be. We instructed the ship's officers in emergency care of the patient, which consisted mainly of preventing aspiration during what may have been a comatose state. We further advised ice packs for physical control of the fever. The question of a cold enema came up somehow. Instructions about this procedure were the most difficult to relay to the Chinese radio officer whose rudimentary English was flavored with American four-letter words he had presumably picked up from some remote association with American GIs in Asia. In any case, we kept in contact and guided the vessel into port and proceeded to disembark the Captain. By this time, it was about 2 a.m. Ships never arrive on schedule it seems. Four hours estimated arrival could mean eight or ten hours. The Chinese, on this vessel, had in fact arrived more precisely on schedule than ordinarily.

Even without sophisticated diagnostic equipment we could tell that the situation was desperate. My lab technician had called to say that he could not get a white cell count because when he diluted the specimen, there were still too many cells for him to count. He asked me to come down and do something about the reagent. That in itself was a clue. To an experienced clinician, that would give away the diagnosis. My senior technician would have told me that the white count was over 200,000, mostly polymorphs, a category of white blood cells recognized for their ability to fight infections; but over the years, I had learned to save my best shift for the mornings and really important emergencies. The chap on the 11p.m. to 7a.m. shift had served his function admirably just by letting me know that something was unusual.

Captain Pei was indeed found to have chronic myelogenous leukemia and this was an apparent hemorrhagic crisis. His emergency management included the liberal use of steroids and blood transfusion, as well as fluid replacement. My consultant internist added allopurinol to this regime, and we started Busulfan, an anti-cancer chemotherapy drug.

As he recovered from his acute distress, it was apparent that Captain Pei was a very gracious man, one of those rare human beings capable of enduring inordinate suffering while being more concerned for the welfare of those who seek to relieve his misery. He was easily the most popular patient on the ward during his stay with us.

A number of telex messages and telephone calls from his home office in Taiwan and the head office in Copenhagen established for us that he was no ordinary man. The company president and several other senior staff members took it upon themselves to request that special attention be given to the Captain. When I suggested that he would be repatriated, accompanied by one of our nurse technicians as soon as he was able to fly, the company representative in Copenhagen and the president at his homeport of Taipei made the unusual request that I should personally escort him, regardless of cost. It was further suggested, if I could not travel, they would fly out a senior medical officer from Taiwan or Denmark to accompany Captain Pei.

Besides the desire to be of service to this fine gentleman, there was also the inducement of the possibility of travel to the Orient, which I found intriguing. So, we proceeded to make arrangements for the emergency evacuation. In such cases there is always delicate balancing and timing. If we waited too long in Monrovia for an improvement that did not materialize, we might have the extremely unpleasant task of accompanying a patient who would die in flight. If the patient died before he could be evacuated, you had failed before you started. Dying in flight was an unusual occurrence, but it had happened before creating a whole battery of technical and international legal complications. On the other hand, if we gambled and evacuated the patient prematurely, the end result might be the same. That, to me, would be a more forgivable turn of events.

Having no specific expertise about all the problems associated with air evacuation, it was a matter of clinical judgment. By the time that I met Captain Pei, I had come to realize that the principal problems one encountered in these cases involved anemia and dehydration. With the pressurized cabins of modern transcontinental jets, many of the more formidable problems of an earlier age were now things of the past.

We prepared to evacuate the Captain to Taiwan with a refueling stopover in Copenhagen. The planned itinerary would take us through Tashkent in the Soviet Union, then to Bangkok, and then on to Hong Kong and finally Taipei. As it turned out, the stopover in Copenhagen was a godsend. The patient's condition took a rather unexpected turn for the worse, and we soon found ourselves in the very predicament I had tried to avoid. There is no doubt in my mind that he could not have survived the airlift from that point. There were now symptoms of gastrointestinal hemorrhage, and although fever did not return, his general condition was decidedly critical. I decided to disembark and seek admission for Captain Pei into a local hospital. Even without first contacting the Captain's Copenhagen office, I was pleasantly surprised to find the hospital authorities very accommodating and cooperative. My only professional identification was my membership card in the American College of Surgeons – but that was all I needed to get senior staff privileges. I was assigned a senior resident or fellow who assisted in the emergency care of my patient with all the concern and solicitude I might have expected from the house staff at any American university hospital.

We continued the same line of treatment, but apparently, what the Captain needed most was more platelets. He had developed thrombocytopenia, a disorder in which there is a lower than normal number of platelets in the blood. There was no way I could have gotten a platelet fraction in Monrovia. The closest I could have come would have been fresh whole blood. That might have been good enough, but this was even better! After several transfusions, Captain Pei was patched up and declared fit to continue the journey. We had been delayed for a week. It was good that we had taken the time for repair; because when we took off in the harsh February weather, on the day we left, it was impossible to land in Tashkent. Too much snow. Our flight was diverted to Moscow.

Although I am sure it was not contrived, the brief stopover in Moscow provided a most unflattering picture of Russian inhospitality. For no apparent reason, passengers from our flight were herded into an isolation section of the airport, past a column of helmeted, rifle-toting young soldiers, most of whom appeared to be teenagers. No one was allowed to leave even to purchase a postcard. And while not many words were exchanged, there was no mistaking the mood of hostility. Orders were barked out; and if gestures meant anything, they conveyed the distinct impression that we were either unwelcome, as a matter of principle, or we had transgressed in some manner unknown to us.

Mercifully, the stopover lasted only long enough for refueling and deicing. Within two hours we were back on board the plane, this time passing through a column of very muscular young women who were shoveling the remnants of snow left by the huge plows that had just passed on the runway. I kept thinking that if I had known how little we would see, I would have elected to remain aboard the plane with my patient who had been comfortably dozing on his stretcher. But I had been eager to see! To see anything in Russia.

Back on the plane, I tried to get some explanation for our cold, and less than friendly reception in Russia from our hostesses and one of the flight officers. The explanation I received was that, for this place, the behavior was not at all unusual. Our principal transgression was in making an unscheduled stop at a time when anything unexpected was greeted with suspicion. The rest of our trip to Bangkok and beyond was without comparison. Only those who have had the pleasure of the personal attentions of an Asian hostess can fully appreciate this compliment.

Lessons

In addition to the adventures of medical evacuations, I have other memories of life at the Clinic. Of the entire range of emotions one can experience, it is difficult to say which ones affect us most profoundly. Certainly, however, there can be no doubt that among the most impressive are the feelings of isolation, loneliness and helplessness that a doctor experiences when confronted with seemingly unsolvable problems of human suffering whether physical or mental.

Nothing taught to me in medical school, nothing teachable, perhaps, prepared me for some of the most anguished moments of my life. In retrospect, I feel it is incredible that all of this could have happened to one person in one lifetime. I could not have borne the countless sorrows I have known in a yet incomplete lifetime, without having had them punctuated by numerous triumphs. Sometimes these triumphs were unexpected, but always, uplifting. Sometimes they were predictable, but none-the-less pleasant in the utter uncertainty of life and death.

Of the numerous experiences that I have had the pain or pleasure to savor over the years, some stand out, perhaps because of the lessons they taught me. Those that stand out are forever branded in the archives of my mind and their telling serves only to renew the vitality of their teachings. One such memory was my encounter with a young Irish priest who might have died in an auto accident, but who, in fact, survived through an incredible series of fortuitous circumstances.

The image of this man standing there in front of me on the morning that he was discharged from the Clinic, remembering how he had insisted on seeing me personally before leaving, is etched permanently in my mind. I remember the sadness and joy mingled in his flashing eyes when he said, "Doctor, all my life I knew I wanted to be a priest, and I was never afraid of dying. I never imagined what it would be like to hear that I should have been dead, and then to look at the clock on the wall and be conscious enough to put together the time and the date, and yet be unable to help myself in any way." The priest had wanted to say a formal goodbye on leaving the hospital.

The car he was driving had been hit from the rear by another motorist, who had then fled the scene. The priest had sustained a classical steering wheel type injury and had been taken to a local infirmary. The physician on call had said that there was no use operating. The doctor had ordered Ephedrine to keep the patient's blood pressure up and simply that he be watched in hopes that he would recover on his own. That was about 3:00 or 4:00 a.m. When by 2:00 p.m. the patient continued to go in and out of shock, the medical staff had supposed that maybe he needed a transfusion. They had recruited three of four donors and drawn their blood. The hospital had said the patient's blood was Type B. I remember that I was called at about 4:00 p.m. The young Italian orthopedic surgeon had casually stopped by to visit the priest, his personal friend, and was shocked to see Father Thomas' grave condition. My colleague had been frantic when he called me. "Come, please, and help me. I think the priest, he die, but maybe no. That damn fool, Coligliani, he say he no operate. Me, I know, we better operate, maybe now too late. But anyway, help me. If the priest die, no matter. If you help me, if you operate, nobody blame us. If I operate, the priest he die, maybe they say I make mistake. But you, you no make mistake."

I was young enough and sufficiently egotistical to be flattered by this display of confidence in my ability. My considerable abilities, I thought. So, I went. After all, Giovanni was a fine orthopedic surgeon who had taught me how to do a clubfoot. He was young and besides being quite skilled, he was very congenial. I had taught him a few tricks, too, about gut surgery. There had been so much gut surgery in my past, from all of the Saturday night brawls in the urban ghettoes – that anyone who had come through the program that I had was bound to be a master of anastomoses and bowel shunts under the worst of circumstances.

So I went to see the priest at the infirmary across town. I thought of operating immediately. But then, I remembered the old adage that one's toughest battles are best fought on familiar territory. I had wondered, "Suppose we get into a tight spot and I can't get what I need? Or suppose this strange scrub nurse doesn't understand the way I move or doesn't understand my techniques the way my own nurses do?" No, I had decided, one hour can't make that much difference after almost fourteen hours of screwing around like these guys had done. But then, maybe they were just innocent and maybe this Irishman's got something working for him at the Pearly Gates. If he hasn't gone out yet, he's obviously made of good stuff. All of this passed through my mind as I stood there. Finally, I had insisted that the priest be transferred to my Clinic. I also decided we would re-check the blood typing that had been done. I knew I could trust my technicians. I wasn't sure who the original technicians were. Sure enough, when Eve, my lab technician, checked, "Father Thomas" was a Type A. The first infirmary had already recruited four Type B donors. Why hadn't he been transfused yet? He was just lucky again, I supposed. We might have lost him without anyone ever being the wiser had we gone ahead and transfused him without double-checking. At this point, there had been so many lucky coincidences, I thought, "What the hell. This priest definitely does have some connections upstairs!"

We went on preparing for the operation with three units of Type A blood. We sent out a request for a few more Type A or O donors. Soon, we had more volunteers than we could ever use. Father Thomas, it seems, was a very popular figure at the Catholic Mission. We began to operate at about 8:00 p.m. Just as it had happened many times before in auto accidents I had seen during residency, with blunt trauma, there was an irregular rupture of the duodenum and a clean cut through the body of the pancreas. Blood and bile were everywhere. We tied off both ends of the duct lying there pretty. I could not trust my luck with an anastomosis of the duct at a time like this. We mobilized the duodenum, repaired the hole and left drains everywhere including a T-tube in the common bile duct. The nurse had said his blood pressure was 90/60, and his pulse was 120. Moments later, after pumping in the next bottle of blood, his blood pressure was 100; pulse was 110. Well, whoever said there wasn't anything like predestination? After eight pints of whole blood, we closed the abdomen and Father Thomas was already stirring and tossing ever so slightly. The familiar groan through the endo-tracheal tube and the smell of Halothane was everywhere.

For some reason, I could only think of the $50 I had paid for the bottle of Halothane that was now all gone. The nurses never used closed circuit anesthesia. They had all been trained by the same nurse anesthetist who never used a closed circuit! Nothing I could tell them could replace this habit. Somehow, they had a fetish about this, and there was no anesthesiologist to whom I could appeal at that particular time. No such specialist existed on the staff even at the largest hospital in town. My thoughts ran like this, "How can you pay $50 for materials, work like hell for four hours and then charge $25 for the service." This was something I had not been taught in America. And, I had no hospital administrator. I frequently thought that if I had an administrator that was really good, I would not be able to afford him or her. So, we just played everything by ear. The main thing going for my establishment was the team of nurses, technicians and secretaries fiercely proud of the venture we had started and firmly loyal to their chief - yours truly.

I have a vivid memory of what happened immediately after we operated on Father Thomas. After we completed the operation, Father Thomas had been rudely dashed into bed by two stretcher boys struggling under the weight of his six foot, 200 pound frame. It was the only means we had of conveying him from the operating room to his bed. We had not yet achieved the status of a recovery room at that time. The priest had gone out like a light. "Quick!" "Carotid pulse!" "Nothing." Giovanni had flung his large frame upon the bed like a cat and started a closed massage. I was blowing into the endo-tracheal tube like a maniac. It couldn't have been more than two minutes, but it seemed like an eternity before Father Thomas began to breathe on his own again. We had a pulse. By definition, he had definitely had a cardiac arrest and he had, apparently, survived it! We had no respirator, and nobody within 1,000 miles could do arterial blood gases or electrolytes at that point in time. In fact, very few doctors in this region had ever heard of such determinations.

Six days later when I pulled out the last rubber drains, the priest had told me the story of his lying in the original infirmary watching the clock while Dr. Coligliani, puzzled by his stamina, had sent for the Archbishop to say last rites. It was the thought of a fake finality that made him weep on my shoulder the morning he told me this. He had said, "I have no money. I am a poor man, as you know. The church will pay for your services, but I wish to personally give you all the money that I own and God will bless you." Tough guy that I was, being as profane of speech as any seaman when I wished to be, I was humbled and grateful beyond words. I broke down and wept uncontrollably with this Irish priest who was little more than a stranger to me. Very seldom in my life have I been so moved; yet I was faintly embarrassed. I would never have let the nurses know that this had happened. Me? Cry? As often as I have told this story, this is the first time I've included the part in which I sobbed like a baby or a damned fool.

In any event, this was the source of the $25 that the priest had pulled from his cassock and tearfully pressed into my hand that morning. I had taken these crumpled bills and gone out in search for some token I could buy. It seemed to me that a clock would be a fine symbol. I found a clock at a local store, but the crystal had been slightly damaged. It was worth considerably more than $25. The German salesman said he would give it to me at a reduced price of something like $60. I told him that for reasons much too complicated to relate, I had to have this clock for exactly $25 and no more. After some thought and gentle haggling, he relented. "You can have it for that," he said. This is the clock I had installed on our operating room wall with the cracked crystal. For twenty years it has kept perfect time and it remains, until this day, a reminder of the things it denotes. It denotes our utter helplessness, and the inadequacy of our own efforts as well as the complete control over all of us of a higher being. Without much pretense to piety, I believe that this clock is a special symbol and reminder of all these things. It makes me think of Father Thomas and my colleague, Giovanni. If I ever start feeling really smart, it reminds me that I shall never be smart enough to predict the death of anyone with precision.

In the early days at the Clinic, there were many long nights. In fact, there were many interminable days and nights that ran together in a seemingly never-ending series. There was seldom time to go home after a particularly hectic major surgery, since if I left, there was no one capable of recognizing some signs of distress in a patient in the immediate postoperative period. I had learned long since that it was more important to have the rest of my team well rested and sharp. I had the prerogative of walking out and stealing a nap at any time there was a lull in activity; whereas, they were obligated to work by the clock and in shifts. So, over the years, I acquired the ability to fall asleep on demand and to wake up whenever I needed to. I didn't seem to suffer any adverse health from this mode of living. The greatest hazard was to my family. But being in Liberia, where the extended family system operated, the hardship upon my wife was not nearly as bad as it might have been in America. Furthermore, we had three children by then including one born at our very own Clinic, and they fully occupied most of my wife's waking hours. So perhaps, there was some benefit in my being away. At least, that was the way I rationalized it! Between deliveries or other night cases, I frequently dozed or thought about some of my lighter moments in the practice of medicine. Just like one particular night.

This young Arab girl came in with what appeared to be gallstones. She was faintly jaundiced, and had pain and tenderness right where it was supposed to be. With the rather limited laboratory tests at our disposal, we had concluded that she probably had gallstones. I decided to perform exploratory surgery on her because she seemed to have developed an empyema or internal abscess of the gall bladder. When I opened, nothing was familiar except the distended, weird-looking gall bladder. I knew it was abnormal pathology, but nothing I had seen in six years of residency looked like this, and at times like those, I always imagined the voice of my old Chief and greatest mentor. He would say, "If you know the human anatomy, and if you know how the organs are supposed to work, hell, you can do anything!"

Well, it wasn't always that simple, but the Chief had been a master of understatement and simplification. His homespun philosophy still came in handy in many instances. As I wondered what the problem might be, while exploring the inferior surface of my patient's liver, there was this slightly fluctuant area that I touched possibly a little less delicately than I should have. In a moment, I realized that I had just opened an ecchino-coccal cyst of the liver, the first one that I had seen in real life! As the little cystic blebs popped out, there was no question of what they were based on the textbooks I had read. I was taken back many years in my mind to the time "these little fellows" had been described by a tiny West Indian pathologist who had taught us in medical school. Like an old pro, I soon had the area packed away and the cyst evacuated. The cavity, I swabbed with saline solution of formaldehyde. Nowhere had I read of the utterly frightening experience of seeing the entire right lobe of the liver reduced to a mere shell. I could only wonder what would happen as I closed up. As it turned out, the patient recovered without complications. A minimal pleural reaction on the right side had resolved with no specific treatment. If I could have seen into the future, I would have known that two years later, I would find the liver completely regenerated as though nothing had ever happened. I would also have known that I would feel a trace of guilt at performing a caesarean section on the same patient two years later for the ostensive reason of prolonged labor. But I knew that the primary indication was my desire to have a second look at that liver. Well, it didn't hurt her, and besides, the rules could be justifiably bent in the interest of scientific curiosity, couldn't they?

It is only in retrospect that I recognize the accomplishments and the staggering obstacles that young professionals overcame to get where we were in Liberia in 1980. In this insight lies the crux of our despondency and disillusionment at being separated from the dreams of a lifetime through the artifice and the rhetoric of a revolution that never should have taken the crazy ricochet that it took. After wreaking so much havoc and human misery, the "revolution" seems to be spinning hopelessly toward a "nowhere" that is charted not so much by cunning Machiavellian characters, as it is by a bunch of ignorant youth who know how to hate, not having the slightest historical perspective that could temper their venom. Looking at the plight of our neighbors does not assuage our distress. It may be true that each man thinks his own situation peculiar. The sad truth seems to be that we all live in a situation where those best equipped to lead are continuously challenged and bullied by those least equipped. One can only hope for more hopeful signs in the future.

Jamba's Claim
A Matter of Family Honor

In early 1963, between my extremely hectic medical practice and my participation in several civic and social activities within the Monrovia community, I had not taken the time to make that essential pilgrimage back to my grandfather's village, my ancestral home, since returning from America. Within a short time of my return to Liberia, I had been in touch with many of my relatives from the village who now lived in Monrovia having been formally educated and somewhat acculturated into city life. None-the-less, with the success I was enjoying in Monrovia, it became imperative that I return to the village to pay my respects to the elders in an official way. On a Sunday afternoon, I packed up the family and prepared gifts of imported foods, clothing and cash and traveled the relatively short drive to Kormah. I was not immediately recognized in my fancy car with what must have appeared foreign manners. When my youngest uncle, the current Chief, had received me, his manner had been reserved. I addressed him in fluent Gola reminding him that I was his older sister's fourth son, now returned from studying medicine in America. Uncle Kaifa embraced me warmly. After that, the entire village welcomed us in a manner befitting of royalty. It reminded me of a day a long time before when I had made the trip to Kormah with my mother on a particularly significant occasion.

It was a hot, dusty Sunday afternoon in January 1940, and every able-bodied man in the village was dressed in his finest gown and real slippers, not the usual work shoes fashioned from old discarded truck tires. Those who were recent Muslim converts were punctilious in the jaunty placement of their brand new fezzes. A few of the elders in this district who had made the journey to Mecca and thereby qualified as Hajji, now hardly spoke at all in public – unless it was in Arabic. Since hardly any of these elders could really speak Arabic fluently, they remained mostly silent.

The women too were in their finest clothes. All the Hajja had their gleaming white veils delicately draped about their faces. They spoke in quiet hushed tones, and everybody seemed to be gazing down the road toward the old town, where the narrow footpath led to Brewerville, twelve miles beyond. Three miles farther down the path would be Virginia – where the riverboats landed. But this day was a Sunday, and the boat did not come on Sundays. That fact made this scene all the more incongruous. Any one who was coming here from Monrovia would have had to get a two-cent crossing of the Mesurado River by Mozart Bernard's row boat from the Fish Market Wharf, and then start trekking across Bushrod Island through Bilima, Sumojah, Douala and several little nameless hamlets – to the end of the island, where he would then start up the fifteen mile bush trail to Kormah.

Nobody in his right mind ever did the whole distance without stopping to rest at least once and getting a drink of water from one of the three or four cool springs that ran swiftly along the roadside. There were landmarks along the way. Charlie Bryant's old rambling house on the little hill was the halfway point

The house itself leaned at such a precarious angle that it seemed ready to fall at any moment. But it had been that way for fifteen or twenty years although it had not been occupied for the last ten years. You could find an exact replica of this house in the countryside near Savannah, Georgia, or in the hills of northern Virginia today in America. But Charlie Bryant's house had seen better days. Those were the days right after the First World War, when coffee was king. People like old Charlie Bryant's family had been well to do then. But with the Great Depression and our loss of the coffee trade to Brazil, times were hard now. There was a moral to the story of how we lost the coffee trade. That moral was that it never pays to be dishonest.

It seems that the Gola people discovered that pebbles weighed more than coffee beans, so they began slipping a few pebbles into each sack of coffee beans to improve their earnings. Over the years, they were overcome by greed to the point where it became difficult to tell whether the product for sale was coffee beans contaminated with pebbles or mainly pebbles contaminated with a few coffee beans. The local Lebanese traders had compensated for that transgression by keeping the buying price low. But even that wasn't good enough eventually. There came a time when nobody would buy our pebbles anymore, although Liberian Robusta Coffee has an aroma that is admired by coffee aficionados all over the world, even today.

In this day and time, the journey from Monrovia to Kormah is only ten or twelve miles from the city center. That is the way motor roads are built: the shortest distance between points, filling the little streams, or placing a concrete pipe of appropriate diameter to cross a swamp. But in those earlier days of bush trails and river crossings, it was a major production to get to Kormah and back to Monrovia in the same day. Besides the two river crossings, the bush trails always wound around and about, circumventing every reddish-brown termite hill possible. Some of these termite hills were more than five-feet tall. I'm sure it was not planned that way, but it seemed so, especially when your feet ached and your head was hot, and the fifty pounds of palm kernels, nuts of the oil palm tree, on your head seemed an unbearable load.

On that hot Sunday, though, we weren't carrying palm kernels. In fact, we weren't carrying anything! We had come to await the arrival of the most eminent member of our family, my Uncle Varney. He was Mama's younger brother, of whom she was immensely proud and very protective. Mama and Uncle Varney were the two of old Chief Jaa Sibi's seventy-odd offspring who had gone completely Western in terms of higher education and life style. But they were so proud of their heritage that both spoke the Gola language exclusively when they were in the council of elders, and they both knew the tribal rituals down to the finest detail. More importantly, they obeyed all of the family taboos. I should have said, almost all, because Mama consistently ignored the taboo against goat meat. Goat soup was one of her favorite dishes. But I am not sure she would have admitted this fact if she had been called on the carpet in the manner that somebody was about to be called today.

In fact, that was why the day was so important. There was to be a trial. And only Uncle Varney was eligible to try this important case. His credentials were impressive. His mother had been one of the wives from another aristocratic house – the Dukuly's – and she was a Mandingo. He had gone through university, become a prominent trial lawyer, and had gone into politics, from which point he had vaulted into a position of power in the legislature. Not just one of the tribal chiefs who just sat there, but a savvy politician in proper Kwi (Western) style, and a bona fide member of the Establishment. In fact, although he was a member of the establishment, he also had the formidable political base of being an aristocrat in the Native tradition. That combination was rare in those days, and all those concerned knew the score. They knew it could mean trouble if a man like this should ever be truly unhappy with the way things went. So they handled him carefully; in Monrovia, that is. Up here in Kormah, nobody had to be told who he was. He was the son of Jaa Sibi. That was enough!

The case at hand was very important. It could even have been called an international dispute. It seems that a young man in his late 20s had recently come to town, claiming to be a son of Chief Jaa Sibi. A real heir, he said. And he wanted to claim his inheritance. That was big talk. In practical terms, however, all that meant was he wanted the privilege of farming a part of the 5,000 or so acres reserved for the family, without paying tribute or compensation to anyone. He had walked all the way across the border from Sierra Leone, down through Lofa, from Kolahun, a journey that must have taken him over a month to make. Speaking a dialect of English known as the Krio patois, which is indigenous to Sierra Leone, he explained how it all had happened. His mother had told him the story repeatedly ever since his early childhood.

Apparently, on one of his several trips to Sierra Leone accompanying the Liberian President as an interpreter during those interminable boundary negotiations of that era, Chief Jaa Sibi had been offered a bride as a matter of traditional courtesy. He was much too civilized to refuse such a gesture. And besides, refusal would have seriously damaged his reputation. But at the Chief's departure time, everybody concerned had agreed that the bride would join her eminent consort at some later date. That date never did materialize. The young man said his name was JAMBA. A real Gola name, and he said he was born in 1913. Sure enough, it was recorded that the old chief had indeed been in Sierra Leone at the indicated time. Since the Chief's fecundity was never a matter of doubt, it would seem that Jamba had a good case. Not everybody thought so, however.

Mama's older sisters had been the most vocal in protesting Jamba's claim. Not that a paternity suit was ever a cause for reproach in the Gola country. This was a matter of principle, the eldest sister had said. The Old Man habitually confided in her, she said. If such an heir were indeed a reality, her father would have told her about it at some time before his death some thirteen years after the visit to Sierra Leone. In any case, why hadn't Jamba come home earlier, while the old man was alive? Why only now? she demanded. So, they had decided to call Uncle Varney to judge this matter. The trial date had been set to Uncle Varney's convenience, to accommodate his busy schedule of legislative meetings, law practice and all the other far flung interests he had in the city.

The air was tense with the crowd milling around, and the drummers were practicing on their skins at four different points, all at once. It strained the imagination to think that this cacophony of sounds would be put together later on in the day in an extravaganza of song and dance. Even the Nafais were going through their routines, as if in a dress rehearsal for the big event. But nobody could guess what the big event would be. If Jamba were tried and found guilty as an imposter, what would be his fate? This was not a court of law. This was just a family hearing. What legal force could their decision carry? Was there any man or woman in this district who would dare go against a decision made here today, law or no law? These were questions to be pondered. On the other hand, was it possible that the sisters, eminent ladies and pillars of the community and everything it stood for, could be wrong? Hardly possible! Even if they were wrong, who could face them and say so? Just suppose that they were wrong, and had actually defamed their own father! How would they make amends? These were the questions at issue. It was all a matter of the family's honor.

The restless crowd milled around, everyone ever so slightly gazing down the path toward the old town. By now, everybody was nervous, but nobody would say so. Just then, the figures of four men in white were approaching in the distance. That might be the eminent Honorable Varney of the house of Jaa Sibi. Excitement mounted, but as the forms approached it soon became apparent that it was not the Man himself. It was Chief Blama Gatawey, a local clan chief of the adjacent province. He was not a part of the business for today, but he was a smart old politician. He had contrived to be just passing through at this moment. He would stop to rest, wash his feet and pray. Maybe, in that interim he would have a chance to meet Uncle Varney "accidentally." He would make whatever point it was he wanted to make, and that would be the deal. He might even remain long enough to join the line in the dance that would conclude the proceedings, whichever way the case went.

So Chief Blama came in and was greeted by all those near his point of entry. These greetings were very elaborate exchanges. Translated freely, they would proceed thus:

"Good morning, Brother (or Sister)"

"Ah, Good morning to you, too"

"How did you sleep last night?"

"Well, Thanks be to God for life (literally, There is no rust on God)"

"And how are your wives?"

"They all praise God for life."

"And how are your crops?"

"Good this year; no cause to cry."

"And your livestock?"

"They all eat well...."

This could go on for fifteen minutes or more, depending upon how many possessions the visitor had, or how inquisitive the greeter was. He might then begin to ask for all of the elders of the village by name, including the more renowned of those known to be long dead. This latter gesture presumably keeps alive the memory of the more prominent ancestors. The answers are punctuated by handshakes and finger snapping at the response to each question. The final answer is followed by placing the right hand over the heart and bowing ever so slightly forward.

By the time they were half way through the greeting of Blama Gatawey, the long awaited star of the unfolding drama loomed in the distance. As soon as it was certain that it was the great Varney, the Fanga team, as if on cue, took off down the road to form a guard of honor in welcoming him. The drums thumped in a busy rolling rhythm that was reserved for the paramount chief: a marching tempo that sang out, "Zing – gilli – da! Zing – gilli – da! Zing – gilli – likki – kilikki – king – da!

The women had started shaking the maracas in the center of town and a wide pathway leading to the mausoleum that housed the tomb of Jaa Sibi was cleared. The graceful chorus line shuffled along slowly, harmonizing on the refrain of one of the oldest traditional songs: "Dee – ya – dee, mana jandi: Dee – ya – dee, tomo lay: Dee – ya – dee, mana jandi."

The entourage was soon at the edge of town, just a few steps away from the old coffee farm. In the days before we lost the coffee trade, that coffee farm had been the linchpin of old Jaa Sibi's considerable wealth.

When we could see Uncle Varney clearly, he had been snatched up by a group of exuberant young men, who were now carrying him bodily on their shoulders, half running and singing in harmony with the women. The Fanga team was more disciplined, but hardly more restrained. They followed at a respectable distance of about 60 paces, keeping up the same stately rhythm.

By the time the formal greetings were concluded at Grandpa's tomb, Uncle Varney was nearly exhausted, but he smiled graciously nonetheless, and waved his white handkerchief high. The unmistakable fragrance of French cologne wafted in the humid atmosphere. It was Caron, the particular fragrance he always used. Now he had exchanged the stiff white Arrow shirt and polka dot bow tie he usually wore in Monrovia for a more practical loosely fitting Gbai – a white gown of homespun cotton accented by a mahogany colored design dyed from the plumwood bark.

After the perfunctory greetings, he barked out his first order in a characteristic fashion, "Get me some cold water to drink!" Immediately the young man was at his elbow with a gourd full of cool spring water. As Uncle Varney lifted the gourd to his lips there was pandemonium in the crowd. Sadia, our eldest aunt, the "biggest" sister had loudly shouted in protest. She demanded that Uncle Varney not drink from the gourd. Then she dramatically hurled herself at his feet, imploring him not to drink from the hands of a defiled imposter. The gourd had been handed to him by Jamba, the man who was to be on trial here today. Uncle Varney had spoken in Vai when asked for the water, and of course, Jamba understood the Vai language, which is also spoken in Sierra Leone. The old ladies in their indictment, had ignored this positive point, but had continually cited as evidence against Jamba, his poor grammar and construction of the Gola language. Hell, that was a test almost nobody could pass. But Jamba stood charged, nonetheless.

Uncle Varney stopped the gourd in mid-air, and in a loud, clear voice commanded the entire assembly to be quiet. Naturally, they obeyed. As he faced the crowd, he alternately studied the face of Jamba, and loudly commanded, "Look at this man. Look at him, all of you!" Then motioning to Jamba, he said, "Come here and stand by me!" Then he commanded again, "Look at this man again, look at him, and then look at me! If this man is my brother, then he is my father's son, you must sing praises to Jaa Sibi. But if you say this man is not my brother, then we have all dishonored the memory of Jaa Sibi, the great man that he was!"

Now he turned to the old ladies: "What shall it be? I ask you, what shall it be? My dear sisters, God will bless you for preserving the family integrity. But look at this man, I beg you, look at him and speak, each of you to her own heart. Speak to your heart and you must know that this man is born of the same great man as you and me."

Only then did they notice the striking resemblance of Jamba and Uncle Varney. They might pass for identical twins had the younger not been more slender and muscular, and less spoiled by the good life he had never had. Whatever a more objective paternity test might have shown, in our simple and uncomplicated society of that era, resemblance as close as this, was evidence enough.

Uncle Varney commanded the drums to play without restraint sending out the message to all the countryside within earshot that the play was on! Not a special ceremony. Just one of those for-no-particular-reason shindigs that rocked Kormah for days on end, especially at full moon during the Harvest time. Only this time, they would also slaughter a bull in honor of Jaa Sibi, to celebrate the arrival of another son!

Of Song and Dance and Sex

In Africa, storytelling always involves singing and dancing. It doesn't matter what the story is, it doesn't matter whether it is a tragedy or comedy, or even what a Westerner might call a musical review. Whatever the theme, there is a song and a corresponding dance. You get the message or the theme by how the song is sung or by what it says. Usually it says nothing direct about a single subject but is a parable, and more importantly, you get the message from the drums that accompany the singing.

Different tribes specialize in different musical instruments, and each adopts a different set of drums, or plays the same drums with different effects. Thus in Liberia, the Lorma, Gbandi and Gissi tribesmen are specialists in Fanga drumming.

The fanga is a small drum made out of a hollowed out segment of a log that will fit under the armpit. Both open ends are covered with animal skin, and the skin surfaces are connected by an intricate web of strings tied taut. The tension on these strings can be varied by pressure of the arm against the chest wall, and then the front end is pounded with a crooked stick hammer in a rhythmic pattern. A combo of three or four fangas in perfect harmonic pitch creates a sound that evokes euphoria, and might bring to mind instant images of a corpulent, swaggering tribal chief, half-drunk on the best of palm wine that can be extracted from a bamboo tree.

Add to this the plaintive chants of a Lorma troubadour, punctuated by rhythmic outbursts, sporadic enough to allow one to catch his breath after each summersault, and you have a perfect picture of happiness. The demand for these specialists in fanga drumming cuts across all tribal lines. In fact, some members of the fanga combo that my grandfather had brought back with him from Voinjama in 1920 were still around twenty years later, long after the old Chief had died when, as a youngster, I spent holidays in the village.

Grandpa had been presented with this team of troubadours by his friends and contemporaries, the Lorma warriors, Jallah Koni and Garmai Massaqi, with whom he had been sent by the central government to negotiate a more friendly accommodation in the Lofa region (the northern most county in Liberia).

The sound of the fanga has always been my favorite. As a small boy, I watch my Uncle Ballah Tooma dance to this drum. As the eldest son, he had succeeded grandpa as Paramount Chief after his death in 1926. Ballah was a guinea fowl in the truest sense. After grammar school, he had opted for the good life of a harem up-country. He was a real-good timer. There would be none of this Western education for him. As a ceremonial dancer, he did not believe in too much wasted motion. As the serenaders would chant out balefully, "Noo – wor – Nai, oooo – Noo – wor – Nai!" then break out into a staccato chorus that sounded like an impending stampede of wild horses, he would just stand there and sway from side to side, making only token gestures of symbolic movement with his arms. As the drums went, "Gba Koom Gba! Gba Koom Gba! Gba Koom ziki-liki-liki-Koom Gba!" Old Ballah's tempo was perfect, and there was a contented smile beaming across his broad face, with eyes half closed and sweat cascading off his brow. He was always the center of attraction at these displays, and he enjoyed it immensely. The women, as if on command, would hover around him, mopping his brow and fanning with their head kerchiefs while caressing his ample girth and muttering little adorations, until he figured he had had enough and retired from the circle.

In the years that would come after I had grown up and returned home completely westernized, it was always reassuring to hear a Fanga chorus. Nothing could arouse me more. In those moments, there was the feeling in me that between east and west the "twain did meet." Truth to tell, I had long since lost the taste for palm wine. Maybe the stuff we saw in the city market was watered down and adulterated. After all, everything else was adulterated these days, so why not the palm wine? I had by now substituted French champagne, which tastes somewhat like palm wine but spares you the big head the next day. As times became more prosperous my palate had become more demanding and more discriminating. The champagne would have to be Dom Pérignon or Laurent-Perrier Cuvée Grand Siècle. Some of the appellations referred to the container only, I suspect. But nonetheless, I've never met anyone who drank either of these champagnes and complained later. Of course, like it is with every vice, one's appetite was continually being enhanced, and I eventually would become acquainted with Tattinger, Heidsieck and other fine champagnes. But for me, none of these would ever equal or surpass Dom Pérignon!

If the fanga was regal in sound and evoked images of champagne and dancing girls, the sangba was the common man's delight. This drum is a skin covered hollow log, sculptured to fit between the knees, from which point it is pounded with the open hands. It provides the treble solo to the tempo-keeping accompaniment of the bass drum or Gbengbeh. All Liberian tribes use the sangba; only their pitches and percussion techniques vary. The Bassa and Kru beat out a slow and more deliberate tempo that accommodates the shuffling dance steps of the High Life, which originated in Ghana; or some variation of that dance, which is similar to the calypso. But what they all have in common is a basic 4/4 dance rhythm. The waltz, in 3/4 time, which may be the European man's idea of elegance and grace, is as foreign to this culture as a durba would be to a Viennese salon.

To complete a typical Gola or Vai rhythm section, there is the kpendegay; this instrument is a hollowed out log or segment of a bamboo palm. A series of slits of varying diameters are cut out of one surface of the log and the intervening bridges are percussed with two drumsticks, producing a sound similar to a xylophone.

All drums have a language of their own. It is the kpendegay that carries the message of joy while the high-pitched sangba carries an obituary. A lower pitched sangba will let the neighboring village know that a party is on, for no particular reason, and the fanga announces the visit of the chief to the province.

One of the most remarkable things about African culture, if there is indeed any such monolith, is the complete intertwining of life and art. The Western concept of going to a concert or musical performance does not exist as such. Audience participation is the rule rather than the exception. Going to a play does not imply going to watch a performance by expert actors. It means joining the group and performing too. That is not to say professional performers are not recognized. They are, and among them, are celebrities known for their singing, dancing or drumming. Celebrity status cuts across all tribal lines in these modern times. A fabulous singer, dancer or drummer, whatever his or her tribe, is admired by all. Since electronic recording is no longer the exclusive secret of the white man, there is great interest in cross-fertilization and imitation of various techniques without regard to their tribal origin. But through it all, the fact of audience participation prevails. The concept of dancing with a partner was alien to Africa before European cultures brought this. Once the unmistakable stamp of the white man's dance was made, this form broke into the urban African culture, and it is apparently there to stay. Judging from the youngsters you might see anywhere from Banjul, the capital of The Gambia, to Johannesburg, there is ample evidence that we are rapidly cloning towards a uniformity that can only evoke a yearning for the simpler times of an era gone by. Those were the days when we were kids. Those were the 1940s.

For Liberia the change is poignant. It is both old and new. The Quadrille and Virginia reel, and some version of the Viennese waltz were always there, transported back by those of our forebears who came from the plantations of America. For a hundred years these dances have existed side by side with Zeawa, Gbeyma, and other indigenous dance forms, with neither group disturbing the other. It was a co-existence perhaps symbolic of the larger coexistence in the political context. In the decades of the 60s and 70s both were imperceptibly inching towards each other. There can be no doubt, however, as to which has traveled farther. Today in Liberia, only one youngster in ten can dance a quadrille, but everybody does the High Life, young and old, with or without partners.

The Golas and their Vai and Dey neighbors have always had a tradition in song and dance. Because of the intonations of the language, perhaps, or maybe just because that is the way all songs began, the ballads are recitative tracts, telling a story. There is always a refrain in which the audience joins, and usually the theme is repetitive in a call and response pattern. The resemblance to the jazz idiom is unmistakable, even to an untrained ear. The story may narrate a heroic exploit, or it may describe a simple act of work or play. It may even resemble the calypso art form in some respects. The song may ridicule a well-known character, and strangely, in a song one is allowed to sing a profanity that he would not dare speak in ordinary conversation. I always thought of that as the ultimate example of poetic license.

If in song, there is a meaning, then in rhythm lies the very lifeblood of Gola entertainment. The drummers are equally as celebrated as the vocalists, perhaps even more so, since drummers are always male and singers nearly always female. And by attitude, the Gola man may represent the world's last bastion of unabashed male chauvinism.

The Sassa shakers (Maraca players to the rest of the world) are almost always women. Rhythmic patterns of drumming become very intricate, and are executed with precision that would satisfy a demanding Leonard Bernstein or Zubin Mehta no less than it fascinated Duke Ellington when he first heard them.

As for the dance, the demands of universal participation have shaped the patterns. Nobody is ever too old or infirm to participate. And it is impossible to be too young to participate, provided you can walk. Even a toddler can toddle to the beat, or to every other beat, or every fourth beat. Whatever he did would just be his signature as the line filed by. There is always a line; that is basic. The rhythmic pattern is always in common time, 4/4. Variations from this theme are reserved as solos, obbligato or cadenzas – and THAT is where the experts, or anyone with serious pretensions to professionalism, come in. These solo performances are, of necessity, abbreviated. They have to be short because they are so explosive in character that any other arrangement would spell disaster, like instant death from exhaustion! After a violent spurt of rhythmic variations, to which the dancer responds with equally complicated steps and acrobatic feats, there is a gradual unwinding and slowing of the tempo that finally and mercifully allows the performer to catch his breath. Then, as suddenly as it all began, the dance is over.

The sole exception to this order of events is the ceremonial funeral dance. Here the drumming is uncompromisingly rapid, a repetitive staccato that soon becomes monotonous. There is usually no singing. The dancer proceeds with the business at hand with a serious mien, but no tears are allowed from these (usually) male performers. The idea is to dance oneself into virtual exhaustion. There is a common misconception among outsiders that the ceremonial funeral dance is an act of joy. It is not. It is rather a contrived appearance of joy, or, at least, a mandatory dissembling that is called for by the script. Now, as for the shindig that follows the burial, that is another story. That is the Ball. Everybody participates.

The ritual dance announcing the departure of the deceased is reserved for the close relatives. The closer the relationship is to the deceased, the more intense should be the thespian efforts of the performer. To refuse to perform is to dishonor the dead, or even worse, it is an admission of disconsolate grief. This is a show of non-belief, since death is regarded actually as a promotion to sacred status. Non-believers are damned forever.

Another fascinating use of song and dance occurs at the "breaking of the bush." For the women's society, the Sande, represents the presentation of a damsel to society. In the old days this was hardly convincing, since the age of the debutantes varied all the way from five or six years old to adolescence. The obvious inconsistency has never been adequately explained to me, in spite of some insistent but polite probing directed at someone who should have known the answer if there was an answer. She was my aunt, who was the hereditary Zo or Headmistress of the Sande organization in that section of the country. In fact, she had been head of the organization since her youth. She had just outlived all contenders for the job, and she was pretty much the law until her death at well over ninety years old.

Speaking of this dear old lady reminds me of just how hard it is for traditions to die. A few years ago when one of my female cousins and some of her American friends became interested in the Sande experience, perhaps as a gesture towards the "Roots" phenomenon, they decided to join the Sande. That is, they decided to explore the possibility of arranging an initiation ceremony. Although it should have been apparent to all of us that they didn't qualify, it was not obvious at the moment. So they approached the old Zo. Their first disqualification, the obvious one, was the absence of virginity. None of these candidates would have contested that charge. But the issue was never raised. The old lady said yes, they could join; she only declined to waive the ritual circumcision that initiation rites would entail. Needless to say, that proviso was a sufficient deterrent. They withdrew their applications. For better or worse, it seemed, none who had experience the functional value of a clitoris was willing to sacrifice it. All of which raises the question: Why is it done? The answers are many and varied, and among the cognoscenti is the artistry of copulation, that little remnant organ has had all manner of magic ascribed to it. Well, I was never one to shrink away from a bit of clinical research, and I must admit that to me, the findings are inconclusive. They are at best merely suggestive.

In the days long ago, when there was no regulation of the so-called Native institutions, there must have been some serious problems even for women. It was widely known and accepted that for the men's society, the Poro, that there were certain inherent risks attached to initiation. In the first place, the bush period was for four long years. That of itself introduced the hazard of demise from natural causes including the usual childhood infectious diseases. In fact, the mortality rate among male initiates could hardly have been under ten percent. For the Sande, it was probably much lower, perhaps in the range of one or two percent in the Gola region, but certainly higher among those tribes that engaged in elaborate skin scarification and tattooing in addition to the standard clitoridectomy. This main procedure was accomplished in a variety of ways ranging from simple excision to thermal coagulation. The use of anesthesia was not a major consideration, either. In fact, as a rule, in this culture, anesthesia was always AFTER the fact in surgery. So there is room for the imagination as to how these procedures went. As in the case of men, morbidity and mortality was related to wound infection, probably including tetanus, since a favorite poultice in treatment of infections included a liberal use of sheep dung. The men additionally had to contend with other factors such as hunting and logging accidents.

One of my earliest cases after returning home was a casualty of Sande initiation rites. While it was probably the simplest gynecologic procedure I had to perform in twenty years, it probably did more for me in terms of advertisement than all of the credentials hanging on the walls of my new office.

The young lady had been betrothed to a young, hard-working and progressive trader in the community. After "breaking of the bush," she was duly delivered to her husband, complete with dowry and appropriate ceremony. But just now, she was being returned to the family with the unreasonable demand for a refund. The problem was unspeakable, of course, but essentially on the grounds that the marriage could not be consummated. Physically impossible, the bridegroom said.

Well, among our people that is a most serious matter. Nobody ever supposes that male impotence could be a factor. It just does not exist! As for female deformity, that is no excuse. It must be due to a curse of some sort. So the obvious diagnosis, so went the reasoning, must be related to witchcraft or some unknown curse. This had to be a powerful curse that would create a curvaceous eighteen-year-old girl, with all the protrusions and secondary hormonal manifestations of her sex, and then, leave no means of entry or access to these wonderful gifts. When you consider what sex means to a man in this culture, you realize the major proportions of the calamity. And don't mention other means of sexual gratification. In the Gola country, sex means vaginal intercourse, period. No more, no less. Boom, boom, boom! Gush it out! And that's it.

So, the desperation of this family could only be imagined. After considerable deliberation and debate they decided to consult the new doctor in town. They told me how hard it had been for them to decide to bring this matter to me. It was unthinkable that such an embarrassing complaint would ever be taken to a stranger. To a white man? Never! But in the course of deliberating they had heard that the new doctor was one of their own. And when someone who had visited my office told them they had spoken with me in Gola that clinched the deal. In this language, it is obscene to speak of the genitals by name, ever! It is taboo to speak of sexual intercourse. In fact, there is not a proper word for the act. It is always referred to in parables and euphemisms. Anyway, since I was one of them, and after checking out my genealogy to confirm that at least two uncles had been bona fide medicine men, on that basis, not on the M.D. degree or the surgical specialist diploma, I had merited this consultation.

I have said it was the simplest procedure I ever did. Well, this is not much overstated. Because of many factors, including all the esoteric thoughts that go through the mind of a young surgeon just out of residency, I elected to have the patient hospitalized and completely worked up. It seemed apparent that her only problem was a fusion of the labia minora, blocking entry into the vagina. A tiny opening at the rear allowed the escape of menses normally. At the front end, the opening into the bladder, although slightly scarred, was not impaired. After X-rays of the urinary system showed no abnormality in the kidneys and bladder, I scheduled her for a pelvic examination under anesthesia at the hospital. A single stroke with the electrocautery set for a cutting current at 40 and Bingo! Major miracle! The hymen was a bit more prominent than usual, but no incision was necessary. One had to be careful not to make entry too easy, or that might be considered unnatural too, and therefore grounds for complaint. After all, a Gola man has to show a little macho in breaking in his own virgin. So we left it that way. The opening into her bladder was a little snug but could be stretched easily. And so, into the record went the dictation:

"Diagnosis: (1) Synecchia Vulvae, secondary to remote thermal injury;

(2) Clitoridectomy, residual, remote;

(3) Normal female genitalia

"Procedure: Lysis of labia minora: urethral dilation, cystoscopy, pelvic examination under anesthesia."

With that cold and impersonal notation of medical jargon duly recorded for posterity, we moved on to the remaining business of the day. This meant five or six groin hernias, hopefully none of an exotic pathology; two or three old urethral strictures; and perhaps one old malunited forearm fracture to be corrected if there was still time before we ran out of linen for the morning session. This would be my contribution to the day.

But the joy of this family, the long speeches of gratitude, invoking all our ancestors, and the liberal libations taken in their names as well as those pour upon the ground in their honor; the big "play" in the village across the river two weeks later; and even the return visit almost a year later, with a bustling baby boy who had been named in my honor – all of these things were dividends of the shortest operation on my record to date. It is hard to place a dollar value on these rewards. Even Blue Cross and Blue Shield would have a helluva time assigning a profile to that case if they ever had to!

Traditional Medicine
Or "East is East and West is West: and Never the Twain Shall Meet"

From the earliest days of my return to Liberia, there was always this problem of reconciling two systems of medical practice. On the one hand there was Western medicine, supposedly based upon the scientific and rational application of facts learned from observation of human behavior, physiology and anatomy. I had studied this system for fifteen years, more or less. The hallmarks of the system are objective and disciplined observation and an open mind. There are no secret cures, no secret procedures, and intimation of Divine intervention, when and if it ever occurs, is regarded with suspicion and disbelief. On the other hand, there was what was being called by some, "Traditional medicine." The hallmarks of that system were secrecy and irreproducible results. Divine intervention, while not routine, was not infrequent, the laws of physics were routinely defied (or claims to this effect were made), and the pharmacopoeia was steeped in occultism.

Can you imagine presenting a paper at a major medical meeting in Europe or North America, and then refusing to divulge the secret of your success, or declining to give statistics of any kind? Of course, that would be preposterous! But that is tantamount to the dispensation demanded by those who would preserve ancient cultures not only for their historical interest but also for their beauty, originality and intent. They would thus demand that mysterious reports be accepted as truth. Unfortunately, a respectable terminology has been preempted by many charlatans who, far from being healers, are more closely related to their counterparts in the Western free enterprise system than to the herbalists and bonesetters of antiquity, whose art and crafts have been passed on by oral history over the centuries. The problems with reconciling authentic traditional practitioners and Western-trained doctors will remain so long as there is mutual suspicion between these very different worldviews.

There have always been adherents of the "save the culture" school. Interestingly, those who would save most cultures propose to do their saving from the outside, protected by antibiotics, vaccines and serums, in air-conditioned comfort. Expounding upon the ancient verities is frequently an easy ticket to the Ph.D. degree especially if one pursues this goal far away from the scene of the subject of the dissertation. Intellectuals of this kind are harder to manage than the actual medicine men and Zoes (or cultural leaders). The latter, I discovered, were reasonable and pragmatic practitioners who, like all good doctors, were first and always, interested in the welfare of their patients. I came to know some of these medicine men personally and found them, without exception, smart in the art of medical practice, if not in the science of medicine, which, after all, was alien to their thought processes.

Most helpful to me was the absence of a language barrier. Although I already knew something of tribal tradition, I had not thought seriously about the implications of traditional medical practice before leaving home for studies abroad. There was no particular reason to consider it. Having grown up in more or less in constant contact with our relatives in the Gola country, my immediate family was thoroughly familiar with tribal tradition. When custom required certain formalities, we had been taught to respect them. But we were not required to adopt the "superstitions" that contradicted everything we learned at school. We were not required to wear the talismans offered by our medicine men uncles, nor did we expect them to work miracles if we did wear them. I recall my brother's comment about this. He said, "What the hell? It's like insurance, man. Suppose we die and find out that all that other (Western Christianity) crap isn't true? Then what?" From that perspective, I guess one could argue it was just like going to church. Maybe all of that Jesus crap was true! And since we tended to believe it was, we'd be literally in hell if we died and hadn't paid our dues in one form or another. So, we respectfully refrained from the more traditional practices and beliefs.

The traditional medical practitioners, as one might expect, tended to be more concentrated in the rural bush than in the towns and cities. The bonesetters, I found much more interesting than the herbalists.

Perhaps we had more in common. In the early days of my return, as it is today, there was always an element of mistrust in hospitals among people in the bush country. This is not a strange phenomenon even in the rural Southern U.S.A. today. In Africa, and in much of the Third World, that mistrust is not as unreasonable as it sounds. Over the years the only surgical disease that had earned the respect of the average peasant was the inguinal hernia. Perhaps it had something to do with where the pathology was localized, close to the very important genitalia. But perhaps it was also due to the fact that almost everybody knew of somebody who had either died or nearly died of complications associated with a hernia treated traditionally. There had been the time in living memory when the nearest hospital or doctor in parts of Liberia was several days away on the footpath. When I got there in 1961, no such hardship existed. Almost every village could be reached by taxi and there were hospitals within, at most, several hours' journey. Be that as it may, the fear of hernia was well ingrained. The only fallacy was the belief that small hernias represented small problems and big hernias represented big problems. This, of course, is not the case, as many an innocent soul has discovered, sometimes too late.

But back to the bonesetters. Automobile accidents were scandalously frequent in Liberia in the sixties, and casualties, as often as not, related not to the automobile per se, but to overcrowding and overloading. A single accidental collision, even at twenty miles per hour, might yield up to a dozen casualties, among which would be three or four fractures of important bones. Most of these occurred when passengers fell upon each other, or when their luggage fell on them. It is easy to see how that could happen when thirty to forty adult human beings are crowded into a half-ton pickup truck along with luggage!

It was some time before I could figure out what was happening. There would be X-rays showing six patients with fractures that should have been admitted. By the time I arrived at the hospital on call, all we would have would be the X-rays. The patients would be gone, hospitalization refused. Most of my staff figured the local bone doctors were at least as efficient as we were, and besides, they got results much faster. Ambulation in two weeks in some fractures that took us six or seven weeks to get people on their feet. With a reputation like that, we didn't stand a chance against the competition. The staff was not surprised that many of these fracture victims declined hospitalization.

I finally managed to get some token consideration from my staff when I raised the question of all those cases we didn't get to see for follow-up. I asked if they knew for sure what happened to those we DIDN'T see with malunions. The point was driven home when I raised the question of multiple injuries. What would a bonesetter in the bush do for a patient who also had a ruptured spleen? And suppose there was an embolus? Since we had an occasional embolus in the hospital, maybe they had an occasional embolus in the bush too. How did they manage theirs? And what were their results?

Having acquired a bit more commitment from my staff, I decided to confront the competition. Nobody had ever tried before. Well, before I arrived back home, there had been only European surgeons. Some were curious but could not communicate with the people. Others were not so curious as to what was happening, just so it wasn't happening in the hospitals; a few others didn't give a damn one way or the other. They served their time and retired to the Canary Islands or the Riviera when the time came. Or they retired, before it was time, if they had accumulated the means ahead of schedule.

It had been much easier than I had supposed it would be, confronting these bone doctors. Their complaints were simple and straightforward:

1) Some persons who had fractures ended up having amputations, they said;

2) Nobody ever showed them the pictures we took. So they could not be sure whether our diagnoses were true or not;

3) We kept the patients too long, and didn't allow enough visiting time for family members. Conjugal visits were disallowed.

There was a basis for negotiation. We could start with the positive aspects, I said:

1) We would show all X-rays to a designated bonesetter, but this would mean not taking the patient away before seeing the doctor who showed the X-ray;

2) We did keep patients too long. We would try to remedy that, and henceforth a more liberal visiting policy would be affected;

3) We would show them every case in which we found it necessary to amputate, provided they would report every death to us; and then, both sides would keep score.

Additional clauses provided that we would not contest removal from the hospital of any undisplaced closed fracture of the lower extremity. We only insisted that we assure ourselves that there were no other associated injuries. In exchange, they would not treat any fractures involving a joint or even near a joint, and all open fractures were absolute "No, No" situations for them.

For good measure, we offered to give them the X-ray plates if they would come back for follow-up visits. This meant duplicating some film of interesting cases we would use for teaching, but the expense was minor compared to the goodwill, and the follow-up guarantee. This was a major breakthrough. It gave the bonesetters the recognition they craved, it relieved pressure on our scarce bed space, and it saved us the necessity of re-operating every Monteggia fracture. It also saved our patients untold morbidity and some mortality, I am sure.

I could get all these concessions by silently suffering many hours of harangue and irrelevant speeches and ceremony. Only one who has witnessed the proceeding at a palaver session can appreciate what this means.

The unfortunate aspect of such negotiations, however, is that there were no means of institutionalizing such reforms. My bonesetter friends considered these good arrangements between themselves and the individual doctors concerned. But, what would happen after these individuals left the scene? That, in a way, is a problem that pervades the whole spectrum of activity in developing countries. Universal education is a hopeful answer, but that is a long-term solution.

Black Stranger and Honored Guest in America

During the years that I lived in Liberia as a surgeon in private practice and, later, in my official capacity as Chief Medical Officer of our major medical center and private physician to the President of Liberia, I often had the occasion to visit America. On such occasions, I would reflect, in a comparative manner, upon the observations I had made as a student living in America and the observations I made on these return visits.

It has been said that racism is the most debilitating aspect of life in America, and this is probably true, regardless of whether you are referring to Black or White racism. One of the most remarkable things about America is the way everything, every problem, and every statistic eventually becomes a racial issue. Everything is analyzed in terms of impact upon White as contrasted with impact upon Black. And if it isn't analyzed in these terms, then that is cause for concern because it means that someone has been negligent or insensitive. A logical extension of this reasoning is that there must be a difference between Black and White dimensions of everything. If a difference is not apparent, then the problem has not been properly evaluated, or the sensitivity of the observer is not up to par.

This is such a pervasive attitude that it becomes easy in any company to detect who is American and who is not. No real American ever omits the Black/White analysis of anything. Those who do omit it are atypical, or must have some mitigating aspect of character to justify the anomaly. This can take some peculiar twists at times. It is not merely a matter of positive or negative prejudice based upon longstanding cultural patterns. For example, some of the most rabid anti-Black sentiments can be found among the most recent White immigrants to America. Similarly, some of the best shuffling and soft-shoe practioners I have seen in action have been recent arrivals from the Caribbean region. Perhaps this proves to some people the economic basis of racial prejudice. But for any Black man who observes America objectively, it is obvious that the situation is much more complicated than simple economics. Unfortunately, it is very difficult to be Black and American and objective at the same time.

And from my observation over the years, it is at least as difficult to be White and American and objective about racial matters.

If this is true, then that leaves the business of analysis to strangers. And in the past, some of the most piercing analyses of the American scene have been made by strangers. Gunnar Myrdal is the outstanding example that comes to mind. Most of the strangers have been White; or let us say they have not been Black. That is not surprising, because the majority of social critics and analysts have, in fact, historically been White. But following this very same dimension of Black and White analysis, I believe there is a dimension to America that can best be seen only through the eyes of a Black man. The view becomes interesting if it is a Black man who has access the Black view as well and the White view. In America, this is a practical impossibility at worst, and it is difficult at best. But a close approximation to objective study is achieved when one who understands the American psyche has the opportunity of observing the Black American and the White American both at home and abroad. Such an opportunity I have had, perhaps inadvertently, and certainly not by my own design. It is only in retrospect, and with great care that I can dissect what I perceive to be the meanings of these observations.

Two broad generalizations have always offended my friends of both races when I have made them. The first is that the notion of White supremacy is an American consensus. It is assumed by a majority of Whites and tacitly endorsed by a majority of Blacks. The second generalization is that Black and White Americans are more alike than they are different. This generalization, the liberal, educated White American accepts with modest self-congratulations. The more conventional middle class American White finds it puzzling that this should be considered a compliment, and would deny racial prejudice of any form in the first place, while citing anecdotal examples of his lack of prejudice such as, "some of my best friends are Black" or "the best friend I ever had in grade school was Black" or "a Black neighbor I had that was the best friend you ever wanted to know, etc. etc…" The most conservative and fundamentalist White American, like his Black counterpart, is unalterably prejudiced and does not deny it.

Middle class Black Americans are, by contrast, not a homogenous group. But it would be offensive to most of them to press this observation. Beliefs, naturally, tend to be more related to cultural background and are only modified by education. So there are many educated, middle class Blacks whose cultural backgrounds do not match their academic degrees. Among this group are those who are more tolerant and those who are firmly prejudiced towards Whites. But solidarity is a badge that the Black man in America has been forced to recognize if not accept in his personal life. It is a sensible attitude and it is also expedient. The common enemy always tended to view all Blacks with equal disfavor. Even today, the prototype redneck is not likely to interview a Black person before offering him an insult. He goes strictly by superficial appearances. Thus, in 1968, a Ph.D. nuclear physicist, who drives through the Mississippi Delta, dressed in jeans, with an afro and a beard was just as likely to be disrespected by the White highway patrolman as a clean-shaven dude from the Bronx who could be a junkie. Things may have changed somewhat in the South since the 1960s, but across America, negative stereotyping of Black men is still rampant.

The hardcore redneck is not the only one out of line. A fellow member of the medical society at a meeting on Hilton Head Island could walk right by the White maitre d' and ask a Black participant, who has just delivered a paper, to go get more coffee cups during the coffee break. His embarrassment at discovering the mistaken identity is painful; but it becomes devastating when the fellow participant answers politely that he is also in search of coffee cups. In that instance, the clothes made no difference. The rule is that all Blacks look alike. When a five foot six inch Black man is confused with a six foot five inch Black man, the attitude that leads to this type of confusion is unmistakable.

In spite of this obsession with race, the American way of life is egalitarian and by ideological choice fiercely anti-royalist and anti-elitist. But that is not to say that the average American detests these distinctions for "others." They, in fact, rather enjoy them. The celebrated informality of Americans is a first class myth.

Reading the script for the production of a simple reception for a visiting head of state would really blow your mind. On one occasion, when I was a member of the President of Liberia's party visiting Washington, D.C., it was fascinating to sit in one of the military escort vehicles and overhear the instructions for what was to be a simple ceremony of laying a wreath at Arlington Cemetery. The protocol officer, or whoever he was, had everything figured out to the minutest detail. He began in the staccato voice of a military commander, "The President is five feet, seven inches tall, and has an average pace of thirty inches. So that will be approximately seventy-two paces from the line to the tomb. Calibrate your steps so that you arrive at exactly the same instant. The review should take two minutes, forty-five seconds; repeat two minutes forty-five seconds. Ten paces to the left and turn. Salute and then retire to former position."

On another occasion, it was interesting to overhear a conversation, or at least one half of the conversation, involving a minor protocol officer at the Blair House reporting about the confusion that ensued when a senior member of our party demanded a change in room assignments. After taking care of the President, the most comfortable room had, naturally, been assigned to the most senior government official in our party. In this case, it happened that the most INFLUENTIAL member of our party was not the most SENIOR official by rank. But, he had demanded to be treated as such, and he was not a fellow who took "no" for an answer. Everybody on our side knew that. But protocol dictated otherwise, and the U.S. State Department was not about to yield on this clear-cut matter. It was amusing to watch the drama, but appalling to hear all the acrimonious verbal exchange. In the end our man handled it in the way he usually handled things like this. He invaded the senior secretary's suite, and had his luggage switched, removing the senior secretary to the room that had been assigned to him. The U.S. protocol went down swinging, but not without a word of encouragement from headquarters. In a moment of profound frustration came the message, "Roger, Roger, I copy. Let the bastards do it their way – Okay? Over and out."

In that anecdote lies an eloquent commentary on American formality and precision as well as the penchant for ceremony and protocol, but not without a sense of humor and a sense of the practical solution to a mini-crisis.

The American's sense of pomp and circumstance hardly ever exceeds his sense of humor. And the Black version of humor is sometimes of the most rollicking variety. There was the occasion when on another official visits to Washington we were again staying at the Blair House. After the evening's formal activities, of course, one was free to undertake unofficial and extracurricular activities. For some this meant visits to distant parts of town. Under the circumstances, it is easy to see how one might fall asleep somewhere distant and have to take a cab home. Of course, if you fell asleep somewhere really distant, like in Reston, Virginia or Potomac, Maryland, your host might feel obligated to drive you back to Blair House, and they usually did. But if it was just across town, the temptation to stay longer was always greater. And that was another matter. Besides, if you and your host were too drunk or too tired to risk driving, then a cab was the obvious and sensible solution.

So it was, that one morning I called a cab at 2:00 or 3:00 a.m. As I toddled out and placed myself in the back seat, I said, "Blair House, please."

Cabbie: "What'd you say, man?"

"I said, Blair House."

"You mean that hotel up in Silver Spring?"

"No, I mean Blair House, 1651 Pennsylvania Avenue."

"Okay man, okay! So my name is George Washington, who're you?"

After a minute of indignant lecture, and a few well-chosen gutter words regarding his ancestors, the Black smart aleck cab driver almost joyfully apologized and drove me directly up to the door of the Blair House. He was so glad to see a "brother" who actually slept at the Blair House, "the real Blair House," that he almost forgot to collect the fare. And when the doorman peeped into the rear seat of the cab and said, "Good morning, Doctor," as one of our own security guards saluted, the cab driver was so excited that he did something that was truly rare. He got out, came around to the curbside and opened the door to let me out. Washington cab drivers are generally far more polite than those in New York, but I had never known one to go to such lengths. Most cab drivers in Washington, D.C. are no longer excited at things like this. And the chance of getting a cab driven by an African college student is increasingly good these days. They would think nothing of a Black diplomat. In other words, it is no longer a big deal. But in 1973, it was!

It is funny how the role of Honored Guest takes on the connotation of the times. In Washington in 1973, being a guest of the President of the United States was a royal pageant. But, the role of Honored Guest was not always this way. A few years earlier in the 1960s when Rap Brown and other assorted Black firebrands were on the loose being a Black honored guest of the American Medical Association was less fun. In fact, it was damn well hazardous trying to get a cab on 6th Avenue in New York City. In my innocence I had violated one of the cardinal principles of survival as a Black man in America. Wearing a grand boubou (formal African gown), complete with an embroidered fez, I tried to hail a cab. After being ignored by at least twenty-five vacant cabs, I realized that something was wrong. It was only then that I looked at myself, placed things in their proper perspective, and decided to shed my foreign innocence and become American like I knew I could.

I got near the curb, and when a traffic light stopped a vacant cab, I snatched the door open, hopped in and declared my destination. The driver was a real mean young White man, with a Slavic name. He snarled, spat out the window and offered a few obscenities, to which I did not respond. Then he decided he was off duty and wasn't going my way. By this time, I had had enough time to get my "incredible hulk" routine together. It went like this:

"Look, Buddy, if you were off duty, you should have turned your goddamn lights on that said so. I don't know what the hell's going through your head, but I'm not what you think I am, and if I can't ride your damn cab because you got problems with Black Panthers, then you better call the cops and let them protect you. If you really want to rumble, let me know. But I'm not getting out and I've got plenty of time."

With these fighting words, he looked back and shot out of there like a bullet. When we got to the destination, I paid the fare on the meter and got out with one parting shot. "You used up your tip sitting at the curb bitching. I hope I run into you again when I change clothes." I slammed his door and walked away into the auditorium to be greeted as a distinguished international personality participating in an important medical conference. All courtesies were extended. Only in America could all of this happen in a single day.

It is in their hospitality and generosity toward strangers that the similarity between Black and White Americans is most easily observed. In this regard, the Black stranger is uniquely equipped to make a judgment. The rules of American society make it so. First of all, let us be frank and admit that American people are basically like all other people. As the old Krio maxim in Sierra Leone says, "Come Wokka, No to come stay." In other words, the visiting tourist is not the same as a resident immigrant. The temporary nature of the tourist's sojourn entitles him to some considerations not ordinarily accorded a permanent resident, who, after all, is a competitor. Yet, regardless of how long one lives in America, one is never entitled to the dispensation of belonging. All Americans agree on that, Black and White alike. Yet America is proclaimed a nation of immigrants.

The rules of American society constitute a benign brand of apartheid that restricts contact of a White stranger with Black America. The White stranger is defined in terms of smaller ethnic separations with respect to nationality or some criterion other than race, such as Polish, German, Italian, Russian or Jewish.

In the case of a Black stranger, however, regardless of origin, he is first and foremost Black. A White stranger would have to go out of his way to experience anything more than a very superficial encounter with Black Americans. The Black stranger, unlike the White stranger, often has the opportunity to interact with both Black and White Americans in their respective communities.

Whether living and working in America as a young African immigrant or visiting America as a diplomat or scholar, the American culture has always intrigued me. From my earliest days as a college student, I have always had a special link to Black America. As I reflect upon it now, a reverse "roots" factor made the difference. I was by name and family background unidentifiable as a stranger. That first barrier was eliminated because I was a Liberian whose Black American grandfather had immigrated to Africa from America in the nineteenth century. It usually didn't take long, however, to discover that I did not really belong. The first question was inevitably "where did you say you're from?" When I answered "Liberia," the response thirty-five years ago was different from what I get today. Invariably it was disbelief, followed by a compliment on my ability to speak English. The compliment was difficult to understand at first. The exchange might go like this:

Him: "Where you say you from?"

Me: "Liberia."

Him: "Oh, you jive ass nigger, stop lying!"

Me: "Who you calling nigger?"

Him: "You, you black mother----."

The fight would be on. Usually a mutual friend would separate us and then:

Him: "Look at this nigger, man! He's gonna fight cause I call him a nigger."

Surprise all around.

Well, within a few months I came to understand this, and I came to know the meaning of "playing the dozens" – that vile act of abuse that Black American teenagers play ridiculing each others' mothers. Talking about somebody's mother, where I came from, was the surest way to start a fight. While I never indulged in it, I, at least, came to understand that it was a joke, like calling your buddy a "son of a bitch." The literal translation of that would demand mortal combat. But you couldn't have mortal combat every day. Moreover practical considerations induced me to conform. Everybody was bigger than I was, and as the boys in the dorm would say, "You got to bring ass to kick ass" or "if you don't play'em, pat your foot when I play'em, just like you do when Count Basie plays'em."

Well, when you got to that degree of familiarity, you were a "soul brother," one of the boys. If you could understand these origins, then you had a special bond with the "brothers," like a cult within the race. The high class Blacks who originated in such odd places as the rural North didn't understand some of these things as a matter of course. They had to learn them through association with Blacks in institutions like fraternities, Armed Forces and the historically Black colleges. In a way, they were as much strangers to this culture as I was. In fact, I had some Black American friends in college that I actually helped to educate on such things.

It is difficult for many White Americans to imagine that there are Black aristocrats. And what makes it more difficult is the fact that

Blacks themselves are very sensitive about this fact. They are apt to deny publicly any semblance or hint of an aristocracy within the race because this often becomes confused with the intra-racial discrimination of earlier generations that was based on skin tone. Whereas the two phenomena may be related, they are not the same. But both are historical. There was always an aristocracy related to the slave society based upon the superficiality of features and color. However, other dimensions of class were related to education, money and freedom status; these were not always color-coordinated. Thus, a dark skinned Black man who was rich, educated and free, within a particular historical period in America, was undoubtedly an aristocrat just as his lighter skinned counterpart.

Eventually post Civil War realities took care of all of these complications. Whites in America, unlike White South Africans, did not assign class to Blacks on the basis of gradations of skin tone or amount of Negro blood. There was no designation of "colored" as distinguished from "black." In America, anyone known to possess any Negro blood might automatically be excluded from certain rights and privileges.

The Black Americans who founded Liberia before the American Civil War were all free and adventurous. But they did carry a degree of intra-racial bias. Joseph Jenkins Roberts, in 1847, was a natural leader, as was Elijah Johnson and James Spriggs Payne. They were all fair-skinned "mulattos" and some people even refined their race further by determining degree of blackness, i.e. "octoroon," "quadroon," etc. E.J. Roye, a dark-skinned, wealthy businessman who became the fifth president of Liberia, was eventually assassinated. At least part of his problem related to his color. He was black. It took J. J. Roberts and James Spriggs Payne to heal the political wounds that ensued. The contemporary press of their day blamed the likes of Roberts and Payne and their prejudices for Roye's troubles. Moreover, from a historical perspective, it is not clear that men like Roberts and Payne were absolutely innocent.

Fortunately for the Black man in America, the majority White establishment forced solidarity upon him, and thereby established a monolithic minority. The fact of that monolith made Blacks an easier target in America, but at the same time, it made them a more formidable adversary in the twentieth century battle against social injustice. The problem of defining class still exists within the Black American community. But it seems to relate more to the White man's values of money and education. It is reasonable to assume that in the coming generations American values will be even more White-oriented. Not only will class be determined by education and money, but also, by how much of each and how "old" the money is. Such is the nature of human beings wherever they find themselves.

The Day Mama Left Us

It was a crisp, cold morning in Washington, D.C., a bit colder than one expected in the middle of April. To make matters worse, it had begun to rain. The day before the city held the Cherry Blossom Festival, that peculiar rite of spring in Washington that brings out the best in those gorgeous gardens in Northwest D.C. and the affluent Maryland suburbs nearby. Really, it doesn't bring out the beauty. It celebrates a beauty that is already there; a beauty that remains long after the parade is over.

Sometimes, like everything else in nature, the beauty and the fragrance of flowers manage to elude the calendar. Sometimes the flowers start to bloom before the date designated for the Cherry Blossom Festival Parade, or sometimes they start to bloom after the parade. But most of the time, nature and man cooperate, and their plans coincide.

People are smart, but not quite as smart as nature. That year, 1967, they had almost guessed right, because the day they chose for the parade was as close to perfection as one could imagine. It was not gloomy like this day, the day after.

We had the special privilege of viewing that gorgeous day of the festival from the air. It was truly breathtaking in its splendor. Having arrived in the U.S. a week earlier to attend a seminar for aviation medical examiners, I was one of about a hundred doctors from all over the world who participated in this event organized by the Federal Aviation Agency in Washington. We had started the seminar in Washington, at the Hilton, and then we had flown to Jacksonville,

Florida, where we saw the splendid aircraft carriers, the flat-tops, and marveled at the precision with which the navy pilots took off and landed on their massive steel flight decks. Only occasionally did the fleeting thought come to mind, "Just suppose they missed?" or "Suppose the hook or the wires that guide the plane suddenly snapped?" Well, I suppose sometimes that happened. But in the beauty and precision of these demonstrations, such thoughts did not linger.

We went on to Oklahoma City where the certification offices of the FAA are located. The grand tour arranged by our hosts had included a visit to the Roy Rogers Cowboy Hall of Fame, a rodeo show and a dinner sponsored by the medical society, complete with scholarly case presentations, and the inevitable steak dinner, for which the heartland of America is famous.

Finally, we were back in Washington to end the seminar and go our separate ways. I had risen early and planned to get a late morning or early afternoon flight out of National Airport to Nashville where I would renew several old friendships. For some reason, though, I just didn't seem to be able to get started this morning. First, there was the immense problem or deciding whether to walk downstairs and get a cup of coffee or call for room service. Ordinarily a decision of this magnitude would not be among my worries; although I do know some people for whom this could be a major challenge. On this cold, rainy morning, I seemed to be just like some of those people.

Suddenly, I decided to leave the Marriott, go to the airport early and have coffee there; and perhaps read the editorial pages of the *Washington Post* while waiting for my flight. I had intentionally scheduled my flight at 11:00 a.m. Reading the *Post* in the airport, sitting there for three hours, when one doesn't have to; these are some of the small pleasures of life. Perhaps it is a bit eccentric, but it is thoroughly enjoyable to me. I would be most reluctant to confess publicly to such simple tastes, however, since it sounds much more normal to complain about boredom during a three-hour wait in any airport. The truth is, for me, it is never boring.

As I grabbed my suitcase and checked the desk drawers for the last time, the phone rang, seemingly with an urgency that made me presume it was long distance. All at once it seemed as though this was what I had been waiting for all along without knowing it.

"Hello, Hello, Doctor! There is an overseas call for you."

"Yes, Yes, Yes, speak up, Hello! Hello!"

On the other end of the line was my wife. It had to be Lady. She was the only person in the world who could have known I was at this particular Marriott hotel, leaving on this particular morning. I hadn't told anyone else I would be at the Marriott. In fact, when one visited the U.S., one scheduled calls to friends depending upon the region of the country one was in and in order of the urgency with which you needed to be in contact. I could not have made any calls until after the seminar, in any case. So yes, this was Lady, and this was the overseas call I had been waiting for without realizing that I was waiting for a call. This was one of those strange coincidences that make believers out of those who do not think much of extra-sensory perception.

But then, Lady wouldn't talk. She wanted to pass the phone to one of my colleagues. They were at the Clinic in Monrovia. That immediately aroused my suspicion. Something was very wrong indeed, I thought. Mama was in the Clinic. She had been hospitalized for two or three days, Sal told me. Considering the state of her health these days that was not particularly urgent news. So why the call? When he hedged after I asked, "What do you advise me to do?" as if on cue, Lady took the phone and said, "Yes, come home." That was all she said.

Mama had been sort of indisposed when I left a week earlier, but she wasn't what you would call sick. She was just a bit out of sorts. You know, "under the weather" as they say. She was not her usual buoyant self. But lately, she was never her usual buoyant self. In fact, it seemed that she was usually so tired recently that her radiant smile was now little more than a faint memory. But, when I left, she was not ill. She was certainly very alert and aware because she remembered that I had postponed my flight until the last possible moment. Not because of her, but because there had been an awful accident in which Mary's little girl, Terry, had been struck down by a speeding motorist right on the boulevard as I was about to leave for the airport. There was never any question as to whether I would leave or not after the accident. It was understood that I would not leave on the scheduled flight that evening. That was just the way we lived.

Mary's family and ours had been neighbors on Snapper Hill and we had grown up as neighbors. We had all gone away to school and were now back in Liberia as professionals. Even though we now lived on opposite sides of town, we were still "neighbors." Mary's child in an accident was like one of ours in an accident. Another consideration was the simple fact that if the child needed to have her head opened, there was nobody else in this town that could do it. And so, even if we had not been neighbors, it would have eventually become my responsibility to help if I could.

I went to the Catholic Hospital, where the little girl had been taken immediately after the accident, and began resuscitation attempts. As things developed, the child was mortally injured, and she died a little more than twenty-four hours later, without regaining consciousness. Brain damage had been so extensive that she never even had a chance. Mama knew all about the accident, and she had been so concerned that she had sent Mary several messages. Mama had wept quietly commiserating with the family because little Terry reminded her so much of Teeta. It did not matter that Teeta had not been the victim of an accident. Every child who died reminded Mama of Teeta, and if it was a little girl, a pretty little girl, a smart child, a well-mannered child, the child or grandchild of a family friend, Mama always cried for Teeta again. I remembered very well that I had kidded her about this before I left for the conference. Yes, we could now kid Mama about this. There had been a time when we couldn't even talk about Teeta's death.

All of these thoughts of Mary's child made me sure that, all things considered, Mama was fairly normal when I left town a week earlier. There was one abnormal finding that gave me some concern though, and this turned out to have some relationship to the sad news that was awaiting me in Monrovia. Early on the morning of my departure, I had noticed little blisters along the course of an intercostals nerve on the right side of Mama's chest. It was herpes zoster. It was painful, she had said; so I had left pain medication for her and told her it would go away in a few days. Now, all of this passed in rapid sequence through my mind as I cancelled my flight reservation to Nashville and proceeded to New York to make arrangements for a return flight to

Africa as soon as possible. As it turned out, there was no direct flight to Liberia that day or the next. The best I could do would be to get one of the European airlines and go via London, Paris, Geneva, or Brussels. Whatever was necessary, of course, I would do it if there were any chance that my immediate return could make a difference.

I spent the waiting period at National Airport and on the shuttle to LaGuardia Airport worrying about which airline connections would be the most expeditious. Well, as it turned out, none of this made a difference. As I landed at LaGuardia and walked toward the exit, I was being paged. Faye, the secretary at the Liberian Consulate in New York, was on the line with instructions that Lady's girlfriend in Brooklyn wanted me to call as soon as I got to New York. There was actually no need to make this call; I felt it was ominous. But I did call because that is what one does even when he knows it is bad news. In the interim between my departure from Washington and my arrival in New York, Mama had died.

There was no longer an emergency. There was no need to go through Brussels or London or Geneva or any place else for that matter. I would just wait for the next direct flight, which was two days later, out of New York. This was the only sensible alternative, and this I did. It seems that those thirty-six hours in New York, when I was completely helpless and unable to be of assistance to anyone, were the most painful period of my grief. With nothing else to occupy my thoughts, I recalled all the years of Mama's hard life. They passed in review in my mind's eye: The early days when she stood before the earthen hearth trying to keep a fire going were as clear to me as if they had been yesterday. I thought of the many rainy nights in those awful days of the Depression, when the only light we had in the house was a homemade palm oil lamp, fashioned from a cigar can or a candy tin and how Mama insisted that all homework be done before dark so we wouldn't have to read by this palm oil lamp. It was not good for the eyes she had said.

I don't know why I thought about these things now. They were all so remote. And the condition was, by no means, permanent. Things had improved, however gradually, over the years. Furthermore, we had never been the worst off when you compared our situation to that of many others. So, I don't know why I kept remembering these difficult times. Whenever I thought of Mama, I always remembered how she never complained and how she always seemed to be making the best of what she had, mainly for her children's sake. This is why I had vowed that I would pamper her one-day, whenever I made enough money to do it. Now that I had enough money to do it, and do it in the grandest possible style – something absolutely impossible to imagine in those horrible days of 1940 – Mama was not able to enjoy it. Worst of all, her body was broken, and she had now died without being pampered in the manner we had all hoped she might be one day. This, more than the fact of her death, was the source of my grief. I felt a mixture of frustration, bewilderment, and profound anger at my inability and apparent failure to reverse the events that led to her death.

As the Pan American jet flew through the darkness, I felt a numbness that defied description. I was only momentarily distracted by the shapely brown-skinned stewardess on board. I remembered that there hadn't been any stewardesses like her on this particular flight before. I had taken this flight often enough. Usually there was a team of middle aged, worn out, disgruntled blondes who seemed to be reserved for this route down the West African coast. I was told that they received special compensation for the imagined inconvenience associated with this flight; and that they actually chose these flights because they had the seniority to be selective. Even so, these flight attendants didn't make any particular exertions, since most of the passengers made few demands. Those that requested anything at all were very easily satisfied. Those like me were not much trouble because we usually drank ourselves practically into a coma as we crossed the Atlantic.

It was typically sort of a holiday or festive mood, and on most of the flights that I took during those times, the bar was out of bourbon and scotch by the time we reached our destination. I flew this route so often, ferrying injured seamen back and forth, that I was well known to most of the flight crews. In fact, I am sure that on a few occasions they laid in a few extra bottles of Jack Daniel when I was spotted at the gate at JFK Airport. It seemed that way anyhow, and in those days, that was just what this doctor ordered. But on this trip, it was different.

I was met at the plane by Lady, and at her insistence, I allowed myself to be chauffeured into the city forty miles away. I protested faintly, but was grateful for the opportunity to get a blow-by-blow description of Mama's final hours. I suspected that the terminal event had probably been unrelated to her hypertension, and, as it turned out, I was right.

Immediately upon arriving in the city, I was adamant about driving to the morgue where Mama's body was being held, and where the pathologist, a close friend, had yielded to my request, against his better judgment, that I be permitted to stand in with him at the autopsy. We both regretted that decision later. It was so emotionally draining. But there was no stress associated with my actual handling of the tissues, as we dissected into her chest. As Jerry peeled away the pericardial sac from the surface of the heart, it all flashed vividly in my mind. The strands of fibrin and the scant amount of fluid that had accumulated in the sac were not particularly convincing to me, as this was not a part of my routine. But later, when the microscopic sections were made, it seemed clear enough to me that Jerry was right.

The cause of death was acute fibrinous pericarditis, probably related to the viral infection she had a week or ten days earlier, and that was manifested by the herpes zoster. I shall never know why this had to be so; and I will never know what effect her newly acquired diabetic state had on the entire train of symptoms; or if any one of the anti-hypertensive drugs had any effect one way or the other. She seemed to need so many different drugs during the final year of her life that one must conclude that somewhere along the line, there were multiple organ failures that were not reversible.

One thing is certain, and that is that in the context of today's technology and pharmacology, Mama's death was untimely. Untimely, in the sense that, under better conditions, her death might have been averted, but not in the sense that anything that could have been done, was not done. It was only in this conviction that I could have any sense of satisfaction. For that satisfaction I had paid with a degree of emotional stress I had never known before, and have not known since. In a way Mama's death was a revelation to me, that my impenetrable exterior was not really so hard after all. It had been broken, perhaps forever.

Funeral Rites

Quite separate from the universal experience of grief over the death of a loved one are the unique rituals each culture performs over and around their dead. In every culture, funeral rites, in particular, and attitudes toward death and dying in general, are important mores that establish an identity. Liberia is no exception. But with the disparate cultures that contribute to Liberian society, there are sometimes strange overtones and incongruent patterns that fuse in a manner peculiar to the place.

In Liberia funerals were always important events, but for some tribal groups they imported some exaggerated proportions. There was a time when the dead, if they died prematurely or wrongfully at the hands of others, had an opportunity to testify silently of their fate and to point to their malefactors. Since hardly anybody was thought to die of natural causes, this made for family feuds and inter-tribal vendettas that sometimes lasted for generations. More commonly, however, the presumed perpetrators of evil were members of the family, so, as things worked out, family feuds over untimely deaths were much more commonplace than full scale tribal conflicts. It would be difficult to trace these attitudes to their origin, since in some form or another they were held by tribes over a wide distribution of the West African coast. Those who lived near the coast naturally traveled more, and perhaps, mutually influenced each other.

Apart from these feuds over untimely deaths, it is not difficult to believe that some of the inland tribes disposed of their dead in a manner more energy-efficient than burial. Long ago there was a striking absence of cemeteries in many of these inland areas. In modern times, however, any allusion to a cannibalistic past, regardless of how far into antiquity it was presumed to be, was a surefire way to get into mortal combat with the descendants of those accused of this practice.

The belief in the power of the dead is so well grounded in African culture that it exists, with modification, even among the educated elite. The most notable and refined form of this belief is that of the dead appearing to family members or friends in dreams and testifying to the circumstances of their premature departure and accusing their dispatchers. In an earlier time, this was frequently a source of high drama. Even among those who were buried from the Christian churches, coffin demonstrations were common. Those were the days before motorized hearses. The coffin was usually borne by four men upon their shoulders. As they approached the cemetery, suddenly they began struggling, sometimes running backwards or in circles. Sometimes the demonstration lasted for hours.

There was no rational explanation as to why this phenomenon only happened among some tribal groups. It would, in fact, have been unthinkable to have this happen among people who had a tradition of Christianity for several generations. Not that they were less superstitious; but they kept their fantasies more in check. The explanation offered by those who understood the besieged coffins was logical, if you believed in ghosts and supernatural powers of the dead. The theory was that the poor victim, about to be buried, was protesting his fate. Besides resenting his premature consignment to the grave, he or she was giving testimony that was considered unimpeachable as to who had caused his or her untimely demise. This involved running towards that person, usually a member of his family, and sometimes knocking down the accused and trampling him or her. If the accused knew that he or she was a suspect and decided not to attend the funeral, the funeral procession might conveniently pass by the home of the suspect. In that case, the struggle would ensue as the cortège passed by. The fact of the suspect staying at home would be construed as powerful evidence of guilt. It was a trial by ordeal generally dictated by the most powerful member of the bereaved family who had hired the pallbearers in the first place and given them instructions.

The situation was not without humor. Sometimes, even the most powerful member of the family, who had hired the pallbearers, was attacked. One never knew just how intricate these family intrigues could become. It depended on who had died and how unexpected the death had been. The more unexpected the death, of course, the wilder the charges. And, the pallbearers could always be counted upon for a bit of originality, since they were, without exception, very drunk. They had to be stoned to perform that kind of chore. In those days the art and science of embalming had yet to reach us and the stench that issued from the coffins frequently required a powerful neutralizer.

This phenomenon of moving the dead was not taken lightly by some of our mentors such as the missionaries who taught us. As long as these superstitions persisted, they could never be sure they had genuine converts. Back in the 1940s, when the Yale man polled our class and failed to get a universal condemnation of the practice of the struggling coffin, he was crestfallen. He could not get any local people to carry out his experiment to disprove the theory of the dead having powers; and, if he had used only other missionaries, he would have proved nothing. The argument would simply have been made that since this was African science, the "juju" would not work for White people. Disproving African science is always a no-win proposition in Africa.

Over the years there has been a curious change to all this with the advent of embalming and motorized hearses. The arrival of these amenities has led to fading memories of the wrestling cadavers. I recently overheard a lively discussion on the subject of ghosts by two patrons at a bar in Monrovia. The learned opinion of my sober friend was something to the effect that formaldehyde, used in the process of embalming, is known to have a devastating effect upon ghosts. It kills them dead on contact. To substantiate his theory he cited the fact that nobody in recent memory had heard of anyone being chased by a ghost even though people now passed right through the main cemetery at all hours of the night. My tipsy friend reminded the sober one that there were a hell of a lot of old ghosts, that had not been embalmed, in the same cemetery. How come they too had given up the chase? Well, that could be explained, my sober friend allowed. How could you expect an old ghost to keep pace with modern technology and the automobiles used today? Furthermore, if you truly believe in ghosts you must realize that with death, there is a freeze on all earthly types of development even though the ghost continues to live. Old ghosts like those of Joseph Jenkins Roberts or Old King Peter could only travel by foot, why would they chase a car? The net result of that evening's debate at the bar was that we would all resolve to write into our last will and testament that we object to being embalmed at death, just in case!

Another curious development in the death and burial business over the years was the practice of having a band and a military escort at funerals. Since, by law all males from age sixteen were liable for service in the militia, it was never difficult, in Liberia, to contrive a military record of sorts that would entitle the deceased to an escort whether it was one squad or a whole battalion. If one was a government official, particularly a high official, there was no need to fudge on the military record, the military escort was automatic. The wives of high-ranking officials were also entitled to this honor.

If you weren't too fussy about the military escort aspect, anybody could have a band. First, there were all the lodges and fraternities that paraded at the funerals of their members. It seemed, in fact, that attendance at the burial of members was the principal *raison d'etre* of many of these societies. If you listened to the public announcements, attendance at these ceremonies was taken very seriously. The notices read something like this: "The Noble Grand So and So of Such and Such an Order commands all brothers and sisters to perform their ritual duties at the funeral of Brother or Sister So and So. Failure to comply will entail a fine of so much and so much and said offenders will be dealt with according to strict disciplinary measures." The size of the fine and the brevity of the announcement would indicate the prominence of the particular fraternal order. The fine was in direct proportion to the social importance; but the length of the announcement was inversely related to the social standing. The shorter the notice, the more seriously it would need to be taken.

Having a good funeral is a mark of social importance. A well-attended funeral, with a large number of floral designs and testimonials from all social and professional organizations in which the deceased held membership, were all marks of importance. In the years before traffic jams were known it was also a status symbol to have a number of cars in the funeral procession. More recently, when owning a car ceased to be any big deal, it became more of a status symbol to honor the dead by walking to the cemetery and having the chauffeur meet you there. As it is with all status games, however, the rules are constantly changing so that the lower end of the society never catches up with the higher end. So it is that in the gradual homogenizing of Liberian culture, the simple tribal expediency of burial before the next sunrise for Muslims and non-Muslims alike, was abandoned in favor of the Americo-Liberian style of wake keeping for several nights eventually culminating in a church funeral complete with a band and military escort, if it could be weaseled by any contrivance or claim to position.

The Americo-Liberian wake itself was a caricature copy of the old South long since abandoned in America while it was embellished into a strange amalgam of African Americana in Liberia. The tribal variation on these ceremonies was worthy of the best theater. If you can imagine combining "professional mourners" in the traditional African sense with a spirited, fundamentalist, tear-jerking sermon, at the end of which you then have a procession of men and women in formal dress preceded by a quasi-military marching band, eventually returning from the cemetery to the strains of a lilting African Highlife tune, if you can imagine all of these things co-existing, then you will have a clear picture of one little aspect of East meeting West. That is Liberia!

Liberia – In Historical Perspective

No one heard very much about Liberia before the bloody *coup d'etat* of April 1980 and the circus of public executions ten days later in full view of the world press, complete with satellite transmission of television signals that shocked the world. Since then, there have been stories of a hand-full of Black men who successfully oppressed the masses of the population for well over one hundred and thirty years. And now it was said, in the inexorable pattern of justice in God's universe, the tables had been turned, and the oppressed had now finally liberated themselves.

From this point on the story varies, depending upon the point of view. There are those who saw a popular revolution, ideologically pure, purging the land of a corrupt oligarchy. There were others who saw a mindless vengeance, and an excessive display of the basest of human impulses directed against human beings by other human beings who had been wronged, but not nearly to the extent and nowhere near the manner in which they now demanded revenge. There were still others who saw a frightened clique of inexperienced young soldiers who surprised themselves (and everyone else) by the ease with which they overthrew a government thought to be "so stable."

There was an uneasy alliance between the youthful soldiers who had carried out the coup and a few assorted "revolutionaries" with varying degrees of understanding of elementary principles of civics and economics. This naturally made for an unstable union. There were also a few intellectuals, mainly concentrated within the University of Liberia, who were distrustful of this alliance, but who would rather not risk debate or disagreement in any form, lest they be branded as reactionaries and treated like the "Congo People," the ruling class who were now dispossessed and jailed.

In poor countries, where large segments of the population are uneducated, there is often a distinct risk in being an intellectual. There is also high risk in inviting dialogue or debate of any sort. That is perhaps the greatest tragedy of it all. Because it was this very intolerance of debate, this very confusion of dissent with disloyalty and equating political opposition with treason, that spawned the system that was violently overthrown in Liberia.

In Liberia there was always a reservoir of dissent – and righteous dissent at that. But it was always successfully abated and diffused by a spoils system of political patronage that would have made any U.S. political boss of the 1940 vintage blush with embarrassment. Whenever that system failed, harsher methods were undertaken. But in all fairness to history, let it be recorded that Liberian society was always among the more humane, not only in that part of the world, but anywhere. Perhaps "humane" could be misinterpreted; so let me explain. What I mean is that there was a gratifying absence of violence in Liberia until 1980.

Reports of the execution of tribesmen who were informants to the League of Nations Inquiry Commission of 1930 are largely rumors, so far as anyone knows. No documented incidents of these episodes are available as far as one knows. The dealing and trading in forced labor that ultimately brought down the Charles D. B. King administration in Liberia in 1930 was, without doubt, one of the sordid chapters of Liberian history. But no one ever claimed that it represented anything more than the greed and depravity that it was. Genocide was never the charge. Mercifully, international pressure ended that chapter of our history over fifty years ago. Much more humiliating, were the series of boundary encroachments from both of our colonial European neighbors, the British and the French, in a day and time that saw no moral wrong in colonialism. Also humiliating were the series of petty loans at usurious interest rates from private lenders in Europe. In fact, it was one such loan that culminated in the assassination of President Edward J. Roye in 1871. It is historically poignant that Roye, the founder of the True Whig Party, as well as William R. Tolbert, Jr., the last leader of the same party 110 years later, both died violently. Roye died at the hands of the ruling oligarchy, which charged him with corruption. In retrospect, that charge was of doubtful validity. His 20th century heirs rehabilitated Roye's reputation. President Tolbert, Commander-in-Chief, was assassinated in 1980 by enlisted men in the Armed Forces of the Republic of Liberia.

More should be recorded by way of explanation of Liberia's relationship to the United States. That theme in itself could be dilated into a piece of some length. But, to begin, a casual look at the Liberian flag establishes that it was copied. Its eleven stripes, instead of thirteen, denote the eleven signers of the Declaration of Independence and the single star with five points denotes the five original counties. The constitution of Liberia, which was drafted by a Harvard professor, proclaims the mission of "enlightenment of this benighted continent." The American Colonization Society, which sponsored the original venture to create a colony in West Africa in 1822, consisted of some of America's finest. General Bushrod Washington, a cousin of George Washington, was President of the Society. Andrew Jackson of Tennessee was a member, as was Francis Scott Key. Over the years various governors of Liberia included Thomas Buchanan, who some have claimed was the illegitimate son of the more prominent American of that same name, and Ivy League professor Jehudi Ashmun, among other notable members of the American aristocracy.

This strange outpouring of Christian philanthropy from New England patricians was blended with a strong sense of justice by some of the old Virginia and Maryland families, who had freed some of their slaves or allowed them to buy their freedom. Seeing no respectable future for these free Blacks in the U.S. A. (or perhaps wishing for them no future in the American dream), this mixture of White Americans encouraged their repatriation to Africa. Further complicating the assorted emotions and motives were the more practical sentiments of the South Carolina and Georgia planters, who feared the politically explosive promise of too many free Blacks at large. And so, the

American Colonization Society combined the entire spectrum of human emotions - love, hatred, fear, compassion – in the establishment of Liberia "as an asylum for the free people of colour."

The first Black man to attain a Bachelor of Arts degree in America, John B. Russworm, became superintendent of the Monrovia school system the year after he graduated, 1830. This was symbolic of the perception of Liberia as the spiritual home of the Black Man in America.

To establish a proper perspective, it must be remembered that in 1822 the American republic itself was less than fifty years old. And the official badge of civilization was far from explicit in its characterization of human rights. In fact it is extremely doubtful that Mr. Thomas Jefferson was thinking of his slaves when he declared, "all men are created equal, and endowed with inalienable rights."

Having thus set the scene, it is interesting to examine what ensued as the political drama on the west coast of Africa. By 1847, a quarter century after the founding of Liberia, nothing much had happened. This hapless band of immigrants, many of whom had died of disease in that inhospitable environment, were more or less abandoned by America. They stoutly declared their independence, with an eloquence that harked back to Jefferson's essay on the inalienable rights of man. One would have thought that all the compassion and love of the patricians of New England and all the Christian fervor of the abolitionists might have been made manifest in America's recognition of the fledging African republic. But domestic politics in the U.S. dictated otherwise. It was not until 1862 when America was itself involved in its own great tragedy that sufficient votes would be mustered in the U.S. Congress to grant recognition to Liberia. This reluctant acknowledgment was ironic because it was America that had launched the Liberian venture, and it was the United States of America that the Liberian founding fathers referred to with pride as "our Native Land."

Thus began the ignominious political life of America's Black bastard. Liberia proudly held the beacon of freedom for Black men for over 100 years on the African continent, all but ignored by America and alternately harassed and patronized by European powers until the crisis of World War II. At that time, America, observing the strategic location of her neglected friend on the African continent, quickly seized upon the opportunity to utilize this link in moving men and materials between North Africa, the Middle East and the U.S. via the east coast of South America. The rest of the Liberian story is recent enough to be filled in by students of contemporary world history. But, as any proud Black person could point out, let it be known that at San Francisco in 1945, Liberia supplied the only signatures of Blacks to the United Nations Charter. Let it also be recorded that in the late 1940s and 1950s Liberia was the frequent meeting ground where Kwame Nkrumah, Nnamdi Azikiwe, Sekou Toure, Felix Houphet-Boigny and others prepared for political advice and spiritual rejuvenation. In the 1960s and 1970s when Agostinho Neto, Antonio Cabral, Sam Nujoma and others sought solace (and sometimes financial aid), Liberia's own poverty was never offered as an excuse. She contributed – and often did so sacrificially.

How these hapless Black refugees could fashion themselves into expert international politicians and skilled diplomats with such limited means for over a hundred years is almost a miracle. But how they could maneuver so well on the international scene, and yet fail so miserably at home, is absolutely unfathomable!

On Violence and Revolution in Liberia

Revolution tends to assume its character and definition by geography as well as by economics. In addition to these factors, on the African scene there is another common thread, tribal and ethnic division.

Because these ethnic divisions seemed largely submerged in Liberia, appearing, at least superficially, to have been overcome after more than one hundred years of coexistence, the revolution of 1980 came as a surprise. The ferocity of the antagonisms and the utter senselessness of the accompanying violence have left many unanswered questions. Most significant, though, is the fact that there is now confusion regarding who is playing what role in the unfolding drama, and in the wake of restructuring the social order, there are so many revisionist historians that the truth may be forever distorted.

Unwittingly abetting this process of distortion are the very people who have been the victims of most of the violence. They contribute to this distortion by a peculiar mix of silence, ambivalence and accommodation that are perhaps the outstanding traits of the Liberian personality – if indeed there is such a subtype. Certainly there are indications the Americo-Liberian, more recently renamed the "Congo People," may be such a subspecies of Black people, who are in a way the children of their forebears on both continents: West Africa and the antebellum plantations of America. Perhaps the recessive gene of docility and accommodation from both of these sources account for the apparent mutation. Or, viewed from the obverse side of the coin, perhaps they are merely exercising their strong survival instinct. Only time will tell.

In the meantime, we might as well set some bits of the record straight, as it may facilitate future research and analysis in a social psychological context.

Among the more radical supporters of the revolution in Liberia are a small, but very vocal and influential minority element that preach class and ethnic hatred, and promote revenge, although it is not clear what criteria they use in identifying their target. And, the nature of the "atrocities" they propose to avenge is equally unclear. Obviously, not all property owners could be guilty of political corruption. It is also obvious that not all Liberians with so-called Americo-Liberian roots were successful or affluent. But revenge and persecution are by, definition and implication, irrational. So perhaps one should not search for reasons to explain them.

The simplistic notion that the violence and brutality of the *coup d'etat* and the subsequent executions were in response to similar brutality by the government of President Tolbert is not supported by the facts. The facts do seem to indicate, however, that an increasing familiarity with violence in Liberia was a factor. If there is such a thing as a Liberian personality, it would have to be a mosaic of some conflicting attitudes and contradictions that defy description.

Beneath a surface calm of casual humor and self-mockery, the Americo-Liberian harbors some very definite prejudices that are deeply woven into his past. These go even beyond the immediate past and reach back to the original African heritage. They are flavored by the encounter of the impromptu transplantation into the American Southland, and the subsequent return to early 19th century Africa. Make no mistake about it; influence was not a one-way street. Those that "came back" and those who never left Africa have become homogenized over the years in so many ways that neither group might wish to admit; but that any outside observer would readily recognize. These are people who coldly joke about the "hangman's noose," casually referring to it as "Tolbert's necktie," and yet feel so strongly against the reinstitution of capital punishment that they organize a prayer vigil in protest. On the other hand, a prayer vigil was about the most extreme form of civil protest they could muster when Tolbert reinstituted the death penalty in one of the first acts of his new administration in 1971.

It is true that this ultimate form of punishment was prescribed for the crime of murder only. But, nonetheless, the return of the hangman in 1971 represented the end of an unspoken moratorium that lasted for fully a generation. It is said that President William V. S. Tubman had vowed since the first year of his prolonged incumbency that began in the early 1940s, that he would never sign another death warrant. The one death warrant he did sign as president was the case of a man who had been convicted of murdering his wife some years before, when Tubman sat on the Supreme Court. So it was said Tubman knew he could be certain of that man's guilt, but not the guilt of those convicted subsequently. Now that is a degree of conceit that is difficult to imagine. For anyone who knew Mr. Tubman, it is easier to imagine a more rational motive. He was probably against capital punishment in principle, but he was too cagey politically to admit that he was at variance with the law of the land. Perhaps, too, Tubman may have wanted to keep his options open for the future in case some exigency arose. He was not the type who voluntarily surrendered his options.

Tubman's successor was William R. Tolbert, Jr. Tolbert's return to the death penalty was seen by some as Tolbert's way of signaling that he was now in charge; and that he intended to institute a no-nonsense, law-and-order regime. Admittedly, Tubman was a hard act to follow. Tubman had been a figure larger than life to a generation of Liberians who were born, grew up and had children during his protracted term of office. So, along with the time change to Greenwich Mean Time and other petty reforms, Tolbert reinstituted the death penalty – at least for murder – as it had always been on the books. The first criminal to get the noose under this renaissance was a college professor, who had been condemned for the senseless murder of a very popular Episcopal Bishop and his aide. As it happened, all of the principals in this instance were non-Liberians who were nonetheless accepted members of the Liberian Establishment. The bishop was a Black American his murderer, the professor, a Nigerian. As time went on, the logic and efficiency of multiple executions was an easy transition in Mr. Tolbert's peculiar mind.

For anyone who might still doubt his sincerity, Tolbert made it a point to emphasize his devotion to the Holy Scriptures in support of the law. Many who had been condemned to death had the eerie experience of being lectured to by the President regarding the justice of their imminent fate. This aspect of justice, one might find difficult to explain, but it nonetheless became a part of the routine pre-execution protocol. Over a period of about ten years, there were just enough executions to establish, beyond question that the moratorium on capital punishment was indeed off. As if to reinforce his pledge of fairness, Tolbert signed the death warrant of a close relative, making sure that this fact was not lost upon observers who may not have known the relationship. Tolbert personally lectured his dear cousin before ordering his dispatch.

With each of these executions, the state had followed the concept of old English law, that those executed be buried not by their families but by the State. It was customary to bury such persons in roughly made wooden coffins on the periphery of the cemetery. Although last rites were permitted before the execution, no funerals were permitted. This was all old, established, civilized retributive protocol.

In the African context, however, no greater insult or disgrace is imaginable. The ignominy heaped upon a family by such an end is unforgettable. In the generation before Tolbert's accession to power, the courts had condemned several murderers and two or three political prisoners to die by hanging until they were "dead, dead, dead." But with Mr. Tubman's unstated moratorium on the death penalty, that was tantamount to life in prison. And, with life imprisonment there was always hope of pardon or parole. So death row had neither the stigma or the utter hopelessness that it imputed. It sometimes seemed that because everyone took the moratorium for granted, the courts passed these thrice-dead sentences without much thought. After all, everybody knew what they did not mean it.

But with Tolbert having established his law-and-order credentials, no longer did every case of homicide evoke this ultimate sentence. It seemed that judges and juries had begun to take matters more seriously. If Tolbert's macho image was thus affirmed, so also was the fear raised that the spectrum of capital offenses would now be expanded. As a matter of historical fact, anti-treason laws and emergency powers were nothing new in Liberia. No president in living memory ever had any problem in getting the necessary measures through a usually compliant legislature; and let it also be noted that judges were singularly accommodating to the executive. So there was never any question of legality. The President of Liberia, whoever he was, could almost always have his way – legally!

There is no evidence to support any claim that the death penalty in Liberia was any more a deterrent than it was elsewhere. But Liberia was never a suitable laboratory for the study of violence. Most societies would have been gratified to have as low an incidence of aggravated assault as we had in Liberia. On the issue of capital punishment, most Liberians were ambivalent. In the 1970s, however, there was considerable confusion when the case of some ritualistic killings in the southeastern section of the country came to trial. Emotions ranged from shocked disbelief to mysterious rumors of wholesale dealers in death and human parts. Liberia is a land especially susceptible to rumor mongering. So the stories got wilder as they were retold. Nevertheless, people remained ambivalent when seven accused persons were convicted and condemned to die by hanging. At least, they rationalized; judgment conformed to the law of the land. But there was deep resentment and virulent anger when the government deviated in the handling of the bodies after hanging. For some unexplained reason, for the first time in memory, the seven convicts after their execution were buried in a mass grave by bulldozer excavation in a swamp. If the execution itself was a disgrace, this manner of burial was the worst possible offense. That was February 1979. Included in the group executed were at least two "sons of the pioneers." Now, nobody ever uses this term but all Liberians will recognize that this referred to Americo-Liberians of prominent social class.

When the so-called Rice Riots of April 1979 occurred, the memory of the February 1979 executions was still fresh. In the heat and hyperbole that issued in that riot, it was claimed that students killed during the riot were also buried in mass graves. This I know to be contrary to the fact. I personally examined each of the forty odd casualties that were presented at the National Medial Center. At one point, I had contemplated ordering detailed autopsies, but the shortage of staff soon dissuaded me. Our time was more reasonably spent on resuscitating the survivors. It was not a difficult decision to make under the circumstances. The rumors that hundreds of persons were killed and mass buried persisted, but the facts are definitely contrary. The spare clinical records of those who died are there, and should be accessible to our children and to posterity.

All of this set the stage for the attitudes that preceded the violence that erupted in April 1980, if one accepts the cause and effect relationship that persists in some accounts. That issue will always be controversial since it depends upon the more or less subjective interpretation of the facts. In one instance in 1979, the law, however erratically administered, remained intact. At least the apparatus remained intact, and so there was a built-in mechanism for correction of the excesses of the men who were the enforcers. In the other instance in 1980, the law and all its apparatus collapsed. Perhaps in some distant future, someone will summon the courage and objectivity to admit that the first tragedy resulted from stupidity and a series of judgment errors that were inexcusable. No infraction of the law was involved in peaceful assembly and marching to demonstrate or protest nonviolently as the students who organized the protest in April 1979 had done. A trained police escort and even a brass band might have defused a potential riot. Even the arrest of individuals and crowd control might have conceivably been handled without loss of life by trained personnel. The restless energies of youthful demonstrators might have been dissipated in marching without incident. Furthermore, firing upon a crowd with live ammunition, shooting at youngsters who were waving no more lethal instruments than palm branches, was absolute stupidity and an invitation to disaster.

It is a pity that courage and objectivity were in such short supply in April 1979 or else April 1980 might have been averted, at least in its more inhumane aftermath. Even if the 1979 and 1980 events are not directly related, as some observers believe, if the 1979 riot had not occurred, the manifest weakness of a regime, which was not in control, would not have been exposed to the opportunists who precipitated the events of 1980.

The irony is that many of those who stood accused of the 1979 debacle have already been murdered and along with them, many innocent persons. There are others who survived who know the truth, and the truth is that the management of the 1979 crisis was monumentally inept, and the advice given to a beleaguered and ineffectual leader was exceptionally poor. It is perhaps fortunate that no wholesale recriminations are possible at this late date, since most of the principals are no longer alive. Of those who survive, their memories are as subject to error as anybody's. Thus any debate, at this point, would only increase the controversy.

Finally, given the history and character of the Liberian method of governing, there was never any such concept as a consensus or shared responsibility for anything in the government. And this situation was by no means unique or peculiar to Liberia. It is a distinctly African tradition to accept without question the authoritarian rule of the "Chief." Parliamentary democracy, and multiparty coalitions are alien concepts to the indigenous African psyche, it seems. Whatever success Liberia exhibited in these alien processes were perhaps related to her cross-fertilization with Western cultures. The ultimate failure of this concept of plurality was perhaps a reflection of how superficial these western roots actually were. Authoritarian systems are fine so long as there is a wise and benevolent Chief. But, history does not record any abundance of wisdom or benevolence among African leaders in recent generations. As a matter of fact, there has been a notable lack of heroes in the recent past, paralleling the advent of modern technology and the rise of militarism. The best minds available are not attracted to politics in these sterile and stifling circumstances.

The President of Liberia may have received good advice or bad advice before the 1980 *coup d'etat*, but the Liberian presidency was always in fact an approximation of an absolute monarchy. That era is forever gone and not likely to return. Perhaps the one who deserves the most credit for this transition is President William R. Tolbert, Jr. This may well be the verdict, regardless of whether Tolbert is viewed positively or negatively; only history will make that determination.

The danger now is that traditional thinking will continue, and the military rulers will replace the "Chiefs" of the past and establish themselves as the new standard. The rise of militarism will further isolate the intellectuals. In the case of Liberia, this will constitute a double tragedy, because the patricians who have been violently deposed might have been more amenable to coalition politics than their military successors, who, by their own claim, have greater tribal loyalties and, by default, all of the attending liabilities of this propensity.

Courage and objectivity are needed in abundance in Liberia today, along with a modicum of humanity.

Whether they will be forthcoming or not is anybody's guess. One thing has been made abundantly clear by now, however, and that is that violence, by its nature, begets more violence. That is why the recent political history of Africa is so sordid.

Epilogue

Thus ends *The Return of the Guinea Fowl* manuscript. Dr. Cooper did not have an opportunity to continue, refine or complete this project before his untimely death in January 1984 during a visit back to his beloved Liberia.

Dr. Cooper's fateful journey back home was totally in keeping with his own guinea fowl nature. As ancient folklore says, the guinea fowl may be taken out of the bush country and educated and refined, but ultimately he always returns to his natural home.

Our Life Together
By Izetta Roberts Cooper

We had known each other from childhood. We lived in the same city, I, at one end, and he, at the other. His sister, whom he called "Teeta," and I were dear friends and schoolmates at St. Teresa Convent in Monrovia. When Teeta died at a young age, I went to visited the family to sympathize. As soon as their mother saw me, she cried bitterly and said that Teeta was calling my name when she died. Many years later when I married Teeta's brother, Mama often reminded me of this, believing that Teeta had chosen me to be her daughter-in-law.

Upon my graduation from St. Teresa Convent (junior high), I attended the College of West Africa (high school), where Miah, already a recent graduate, was working in the school office and substitute teaching. He taught me on various occasions and we became good friends. Sometimes he walked me home from school carrying my books. My classmates and I kidded around with Mr. Cooper, "our teacher," who was really just one us being not much older than we were. We had so much fun teasing him. This was only for a short while as he soon left for the U.S. for college.

Miah and I met again in Atlanta, Georgia, where he was a senior at Clarke College and I had come to Spelman College as a freshman. It was here that we began to date. Miah was president of the Student Association at Clark College, president of his class, and prominent in his fraternity, Omega Psi Phi. He was popular and well known among his colleagues.

I remember I had invited him to the Spelman Freshman Dance as a date for my roommate since I already had a date. Miah misunderstood this thinking that he would be my date. Disappointed, he left the party early. The corsage he had brought, thinking it was for me, was the most beautiful thing. It was not to be compared to the sleazy one my actual date bought me. Miah felt I had stood him up, but it was all a misunderstanding. This I made up for later.

Miah would write me notes describing "me to a tee" while asking me to find him a girl just like the description. Although I was enjoying getting to know Miah better in Atlanta, I had only recently met some of my father's close relatives who lived in Massachusetts and they encouraged me to move closer to them.

I left Spelman and went to Boston University in the spring of 1950. Around the same time, Miah graduated from Clark College and left Atlanta to attend Meharry Medical School in Nashville, Tennessee. We corresponded regularly and he came up to visit me in Boston.

Eventually, during a time when my mother had come from Liberia for eye surgery in Boston, Miah thought it appropriate to come to visit us in order to propose to me and get my mother's blessing. Even though he could not have anticipated what my mother's reaction would be, Miah had confidently arrived with an engagement ring, which he promptly put on my finger.

After my mother returned to Liberia, I went to Nashville and Miah and I were married by the Reverend Kelly Miller Smith on July 11, 1953. Dr. Arnold Jones, Miah's classmate, and his wife, Camille, were witnesses. Because we were both Liberian government scholarship students and students were not permitted to marry while on scholarship, we kept our marriage a secret.

I continued studying at Boston University and Miah continued at Meharry. We both graduated in the summer of 1954. Miah had earned his M.D. degree and I, my B.Sc. degree in Education.

We moved to Ohio where Miah was to do his internship at Maumee Valley Hospital in Toledo. I enrolled at Western Reserve University (now Case Western Reserve University) where I earned a Master of Science degree in Library Science. In the meantime, Miah completed his Medical Internship at Maumee Valley.

During our time in Toledo, we lived at the home of Mr. and Mrs. Patrick Chavis, parents of Miah's medical school classmate, Bill Chavis. We spent many happy times with Bill and his wife, Marlene, who have remained lifetime friends.

In 1955 Miah and I returned home to Liberia for a visit. We reported to the Liberian Ministry of Education, presented our diplomas, and formally announced our marriage. We were well received by both our country and our families.

Our visit home was brief as Miah had to return to the U.S. to start a residency in Surgery at Meharry Medical College. I accompanied him to Nashville in the fall of 1955 and was employed at Fisk University Library as Reference Librarian with Arna Bontemps (1902 – 1973) as Head Librarian.

Life in Nashville was quite busy and meaningful. We had many very good friends there including Violet and Philip Nicholas, whom we called Vie and Nic. Nic was Miah's classmate and a true brother. Vie and I became like sisters and she introduced me to another friend, Ruby Smith. We became an inseparable trio.

While we lived in Nashville, my dear aunt, Iola, and her husband, Alford Russ, moved to Nashville with their son Louis, who was a student at Fisk. I was happy to have my aunt (my mother's sister) near me as I had been close to her from the time I was born and she was always very special to me.

Miah and I had so many fond memories of Nashville. We were members of several professional, social and civic organizations. We were also members of Clark Memorial Methodist Church. Two of our three children, Armah (Butch) and Dawn, were born in Nashville at Hubbard Hospital in 1956 and 1958 respectively.

Although we were based in Nashville, Miah's residency program required that he travel to other cities. This meant I would frequently join him with our two small children. Life was indeed hectic at times.

Miah's surgical training took him from Mound Bayou, a small city in Mississippi, to New York City – two great extremes. Meharry had an arrangement with a small hospital run by the Knights of Tabor, a black organization in Mound Bayou, to send residents on rotation. It was quite an experience for both Miah and me because this was at the height of segregation and Jim Crow in the southern states of America. We would later experience the historic "sit-ins" and boycotts in Nashville and proudly play our part in trying to end segregation in the South.

In contrast to our life in the South, now in busy New York, Miah was at Sloan Kettering Memorial Hospital for his oncology surgical training. Because Sloan Kettering Memorial is internationally renowned, famous dignitaries, like Eva Perón of Argentina, were patients while Miah was in training. He was fortunate to have the experience of being trained by many of the most famous doctors in the field of oncology. He met famous colleagues such as Drs. LaSalle Lefall (a fellow resident), Michael E. DeBakey, Harry Grabstald, and Robert M. Zollinger, just to name a few that I remember.

In 1979 when Miah hosted a joint meeting of the Liberian and American Cancer Societies in Monrovia, many of his oncology colleagues from the U.S. came to Liberia. This was during the presidency of Dr. LaSalle Lefall and it was the first time that the American Cancer Society met on the continent of Africa.

By the time that Miah and I moved to New York, I already knew and loved the city. I had spent time in New York while I was a student at Boston University because my uncle and aunt, Roland and Elizabeth Cooper, and their daughter Margie lived there. Uncle Roland was Consul for the Republic of Liberia in New York at the time. During my summer visits with my uncle and aunt, I was fortunate to work at the Columbia University Library, thanks to a Liberian student, Frank Stewart, who introduced me to the university librarian. The practical experience at Columbia proved invaluable to me professionally.

In New York, Miah and I lived in Manhattan at Sloan Kettering Memorial Hospital's Residents' Apartments. Life in New York City was both exciting and challenging. Miah's schedule, as a resident, was extremely busy; and I was taking care of two small children. Parking our car proved particularly difficult. Because our apartment building had no parking facility, we had to park our car on Long Island during the week and on weekends we had to constantly move the car from one side of the street to the next. Despite all this, we managed to thoroughly enjoy the social and cultural aspects of the city.

Once Miah completed his residency, we went back to Nashville where he completed his surgical training. We then started plans to return to Liberia. It was a special time in our lives; we were going home to work and help our people. Miah dreamed of establishing and running a clinic. I planned to work at the University of Liberia developing its library.

It was farewell time in Nashville. There were parties, gifts, plaques, you name it – our friends and colleagues were saying goodbye in grand style. Many could not understand why we were leaving, as there were so many opportunities in the U.S. given our education; but we had other plans. We had various emotions, both happy and sad. We were happy to be going home to start a new venture; and sad to leave our colleagues and friends.

Miah and I packed our belongings into a Dodge station wagon and were on our way to New York to board the ship to Liberia. All of our larger personal effects including household appliances had been pre-shipped via truck or train to Pier 33 in Brooklyn, New York from where they would be shipped to Liberia.

This was the first time we would be setting up house in Africa. We were looking forward to it, but we were also somewhat anxious and nervous. In addition to our two kids with all of their stuff, we had to buy souvenirs and gifts for our relatives at home. We were also taking medical instruments and supplies for our clinic project. Miah already had the picture I had cut out from a magazine. He carried the picture in his wallet from the day I gave it to him. Whenever we talked about returning home, we always pulled it out and discussed our plans to build "our clinic."

When we arrived in New York, I still had a lot more shopping to do. We were staying in Brooklyn with our dear friend Ruby Smith, who was kind enough to baby-sit one day while I was out shopping and Miah had gone to the immigration office for a final tax clearance, which we needed before leaving America. I will never forget that I decided to call Ruby to check on the babies and to inquire if there was any news from Miah. Ruby answered me emphatically: "Yes." I was to stop shopping immediately as we would need every cent we had to pay some taxes that we had somehow overlooked.

I rushed home from Macy's via the A Train subway. I walked in carrying two beautiful side table lamps wondering whether I would have to return them as the message from Miah said we needed every cent. Fortunately, we had enough money to pay the taxes and keep my beautiful lamps, but we couldn't buy another thing if we were to have the necessary cushion we would need as we settled in at home in Liberia.

We were set to sail on the 20th of January 1961. It was also Inauguration Day. What a great time it was in America with the popular, glamorous and talented first couple, John and Jacquelyn Kennedy. We were sorry that we would miss seeing all the festivities on television, but we were all set to go to Pier 33 in Brooklyn to board the "African Mercury," a Farrell Lines ship that was sailing for Monrovia.

On the morning we were to leave, I looked outside and thought, "What bad weather to be traveling. I doubt that traffic can flow in this snowstorm. It's a blizzard!" Just then the phone rang. It was Farrell Lines calling to tell us that we wouldn't be sailing that day after all.

We got our wish. We did get to see the inauguration on television. It was beautiful regardless of the weather. As we listened to the inaugural address of President Kennedy, Miah was very moved. When President Kennedy said, "Ask not what your country can do for you - ask what you can do for your country," Miah immediately commented, "Those words will go down in history and will be quoted many times; watch!" How true! Many times later he and I would remember his observations during that inauguration. Little did we know that we would hear of President Kennedy's assassination and watch his funeral on television in Liberia. Coincidentally, the national medical center of Liberia, for which Miah became the first Chief Medical Officer, would be named in honor of John F. Kennedy.

We sailed on the African Mercury within a few days of the inauguration. The accommodations for passengers were limited because it was a cargo ship. The service, however, was excellent. Our children had a great time being spoiled by the Captain, his crew and fellow passengers. It was a long voyage, taking us about eight days to cross the Atlantic.

The first time we saw land after departing New York was a distant landmass off the west coast of Africa. I believe it was the Cape Verde Islands. We docked in Dakar, Senegal for some passengers to disembark. Butch and Dawn, our two children, were so excited to see the Senegalese people. They were tall, dark, and elegant wearing long white flowing robes. All passengers were allowed to leave the ship and visit Dakar for a few hours. We were fortunate to meet and have lunch with the Liberian Ambassador, S. Edward Peal, and his wife, Florence.

The next day we arrived in Monrovia Free Port. What a welcome! Our families and friends came aboard to meet us even before we disembarked. The children asked, "Are they our Liberian families? We love them!"

In Monrovia, we spent sometime with my mother, Catherine Roberts, and with Miah's parents, Charles and MaryAnn Cooper, before we set up our home and started to work. Miah was assigned to the Liberian Government Hospital as Chief Surgeon and I to the University of Liberia as Head Librarian. In addition to his position at the hospital, Miah opened his private office in a rented space. Meanwhile, I was organizing the University's library by introducing the Dewey Decimal System, a card catalog, books to support the curriculum and a Special Collection on Africana with emphasis on Liberia.

Monrovia was an exhilarating place to be. We were with our relatives, childhood friends and familiar faces. President W. V. S. Tubman had introduced an Open Door Policy and many expatriates were coming into Liberia as investors. Professional Liberians, who had studied abroad, were returning home to work and help develop the country. Monrovia was quite cosmopolitan with international organizations, civic and social clubs, and activities. We got involved in the church, the Rotary International Club of Monrovia, the International Women's Club, the YWCA, the Liberian Medical and Dental Association, Beta Theta Boulé chapter of the Sigma Pi Phi Fraternity, the Social Services of Liberia and several boards, just to name a few. The country seemed stable with all the ingredients necessary for growth and development. Things looked good.

We presented the picture of our "dream clinic" cut out from the magazine so many years before to Milton and Richards, a Liberian architectural company. They had never built a clinic before and were excited about the venture. With a loan from the Bank of Liberia, we were able to proceed. The president of the bank, A Romeo Horton, and its board felt it was an excellent project. As the clinic was being built on the property we purchased in Sinkor, a suburb of Monrovia, we would visit the site daily, watching its progress and planning for its operation. We were already scouting around for staff both at home and abroad.

Finally, the Cooper Clinic was finished and ready to be opened. At its opening, President Tubman graced the occasion along with his wife, Mrs. Antoinette Tubman. Also present were: Dr. Murrey Barclay, the Secretary of Heath at the time; the architect Aaron Milton, Reverend and Mrs. Samuel Smith, Miah's former high school teachers and mentors; as well as other dignitaries, friends and relatives. I was expecting our third child, Lisa, at the time of the grand opening.

The Cooper Clinic, beginning in 1963, served the Liberian and foreign communities in Monrovia as a private diagnostic clinic and hospital for acute diseases. The orientation of the clinic was surgical, including obstetrics and gynecology. At the height of operations in the 1970s, the clinic had twenty-five beds; 24-hour coverage by two full-time doctors, one a certified surgical specialist; two part-time physicians; twelve graduate nurses; three laboratory technologists; three practical nurses; a nurse pharmacist, a physiotherapist and twenty-five ancillary employees.

Notably, the Cooper Clinic was renown for its services not only to Liberians but also as an International Aid to travelers in the west African region. We had contracts with international organizations, companies and embassies to deliver health care services.

I particularly enjoyed assisting in the operations of the clinic. In 1966, I decided to leave the University of Liberia in order to give more time to running of our clinic. I felt comfortable leaving the university at this time as the library was now organized and running smoothly with a professional and semi-professional staff. My responsibilities at the Cooper Clinic included purchasing supplies; public relations and general operations. Some years later, we embarked upon a major expansion of the clinic including additional private patient rooms, a labor and delivery theater, and a Health Club for exercise and fitness.

Having left the university library to be at the clinic, I became nostalgic about my library work and had the idea of hosting a television program about books. I presented the idea to T. Kla Williams and Eustace Smith, of the Liberian Broadcasting Corporation, who wholeheartedly embraced the concept and were instrumental in the production of my television program, "The World of Books." Miah was extremely supportive of this project suggesting the theme song for the program, "Breezin'," by the American jazz guitarist George Benson, and appearing as my guest several times.

For the first several years, Miah and I lived with our children in one of the physician's apartments at the Clinic. Our next project was to design and build our dream home. We chose a spot in Oldest Congotown, another suburb of Monrovia, on a hill overlooking the

Atlantic Ocean. Our house was a split-level dwelling using the traditional cement and rock wall exterior while finishing the interior with Italian marble and Liberian mahogany wood. We truly enjoyed creating our home, that Miah called our "castle," which was complete with a terraced garden and gazebo.

For the thirteen years that we lived in Oldest Congotown, we had so many special moments. Friends from the United States and other parts of the world frequently visited. We hosted so many parties, receptions, teas, social and professional meetings. Some special visitors included Mahalia Jackson, the famous African American gospel singer; Malcolm X; Ernest Morial, the first African American Mayor of New Orleans and his wife, Sybil Morial, my roommate from Boston University; Dr. Jack Lange and his wife, De Lange of Lange Medical Publications; Drs. Bill and Marlene Chavis, our friends from Toledo, Ohio; Colonel Donald Parker of U.S.A.I.D, and his wife, Alma Parker; Ambassador W. Beverly Carter, Jr., U.S. Ambassador to Liberia; Ambassador Julius Walker and his wife, Savannah Walker; Dr. Philip Nicholas and his wife, Vie, our friends from Nashville; Ruby Smith, our friend from New York; Isaac and Edith Roberts, my relatives from Massachusetts and so many other special friends.

We prided ourselves in welcoming a wide range of people of diverse backgrounds into our home. This was epitomized by the fairytale wedding of our daughter, Dawn, to Milton Nathaniel Barnes in December 1979.

Although our home in Oldest Congotown was our official residence, we invited relatives and friends and spent holidays in the scenic town of Calpe, near Alicante, in the south of Spain, where we had a summer home, "Villa Ardalis" (named for our three children: Armah, Dawn and Lisa). In Calpe, our neighbors were our cousins John and Calista Cooper and their daughters, Helene and Marlene Cooper.

In March 1972, I was in the U.S. to receive emergency medical treatment when Liberian President William R. Tolbert, Jr. appointed Miah as the first Chief Medical Officer of the John F. Kennedy Medical Center, the country's primary medical facility. While thanking the President for his confidence in appointing him to this position, Miah also thanked the President for allowing him to continue his work as a private physician, thus maintaining the operations of the Cooper Clinic. Miah promised to do his best, always in the interest of the patients first, while seeking every advantage for the institution. I was flattered to learn of Miah's remarks during his acceptance speech when he said, "I am a little bit worried and my predicament today is not helped by the absence of my best friend, principal advisor and booster over the past twenty years my Lady, my wife. I regret even more the circumstances of her absence."

During his tenure as Chief Medical Officer of the JFK Medical Center, Miah was instrumental in putting the hospital on the international map of medical facilities. His initiatives included the installation of a Cobalt Teletherapy Unit in May 1976 donated to the JFKMC by Howard University School of Medicine. Instrumental in this project and present at the dedication ceremony were Marion Mann, M.D., Dean of Howard University School of Medicine and Ulrich K. Henschke, M.D. Ph.D., Professor and Chairman, Department of Radiotherapy Howard University School of Medicine.

Also during his tenure as Chief Medical Officer, in February 1979, Miah, as Founder of the Liberian Cancer Society, hosted a joint clinical conference of the American and Liberian Cancer Societies. This was the first time the American Cancer Society had convened in Africa. Miah's longtime friend and colleague, LaSalle Lefall, M.D. was President of the American Cancer Society and Mrs. Corinna Hilton van Ee was President of the Liberian Cancer Society. The Organizing Committee for the American Cancer Society, Inc. included Arthur I. Holleb, M.D., Senior Vice President for Medical Affairs and Research and Gerry Ann S. de Harven, Director, International Activities. For the Liberian Cancer Society, Inc., the Organizing Committee included H. Nehemiah Cooper, M.D., F.A.C.S., Chief Medical Officer and Director of Tumor Clinic, JFK Medical Center, Chairman, Professional Education Committee; A.O. Sobo, M.D., D.M.R.T., W.H.O. Radio therapist to JFKMC, Associate Director, Tumor Clinic, Vice Chair, Professional Education Committee; Joseph N. Togba, Jr., M.D., Conference Secretary-General, Attending Surgeon, JFKMC, Member, Professional Education Committee; Mrs. Corinna Hilton van Ee, President, Liberian Cancer Society; Mrs. Linnie Kesselley, Member of the Board of Directors and Mr. Frank Roberts, Treasurer, Liberian Cancer Society.

Perhaps Miah's most outstanding contribution during his tenure as Chief Medical Officer to the JFK Medical Center was the Liberian Health Care Delivery System, which he was instrumental in designing.

In December of 1979, Miah announced his retirement as Chief Medical Officer of the JFK Medical Center but continued to associate with the institution as Director of the Tumor Clinic. His remarks to his staff as he retired indicated that whatever accomplishments he had achieved were punctuated by the number of incomplete projects worthy of completion. Completing these projects would require professional dedication with optimism for the future. He stated, "I leave you with peace, but I hope that it will be a restless peace – that is even more demanding in quest of excellence."

Miah and I returned to the U.S. in 1980 after Liberia experienced a bloody *coup d'état*. President Tolbert was assassinated along with thirteen high ranking government officials including several of our relatives and close friends: James T. Phillips, Minister of Agriculture; C. Cecil Dennis, Minister of Foreign Affairs; P. Clarence Parker, Treasurer of the ruling True Whig Party; Frank Stewart, Director of the Budget. Many families were disrupted and, like our family, they left Liberia.

Miah, who had been President Tolbert's private physician, barely escaped death himself. When we learned the President had been killed and that there had been fighting in the streets of Monrovia, Miah left our home in Oldest Congotown to go to the hospital. He was certain that there had been casualties and, as a physician, he felt obligated to help those who may have been wounded. He was attacked by a group of armed soldiers who beat him up, dragged him along the road and threw him into the back of a truck. He was driven to the Post Stockade Prison and incarcerated along with so many others. Fortunately, one of the men who had seized power, Chea Cheepo, protected and saved Miah's life because Mr. Cheepo remembered that Dr. Cooper had treated his mother and saved her life without even charging a fee.

When we first returned to live in America, Miah and I settled in the Washington D. C. area where he worked at the Howard University School of Medicine at the invitation of George Jones, M.D., Department of Urology.

Later, Miah was invited to join the staff of his alma mater, Meharry Medical College, in Nashville, as Professor of Surgery and Interim Clinical Director of the International Center for Health Sciences. The International Center was pleased to have Miah head the team as his experience and knowledge of the health care system in West Africa would help Meharry to launch a planned expansion of health care aid to the African continent. In addition to continuing its training programs for African health care professionals, the International Center hoped to promote bilateral cooperation in the form of research projects.

Even though we had settled in Nashville, we continued to try to operate the Cooper Clinic in Liberia from a distance. We had left a Filipino national, Dr. Tirad, in charge. I went back to Liberia several times to check on the operation of the clinic as well as our other businesses. Miah traveled to Africa because of his job with the International Center. He kept in touch with his African professional colleagues and organizations. Although he did not go to Liberia, his heart was always there and he really missed his work at the Clinic.

In January 1984 Miah was scheduled to address the West African College of Surgeons at their meeting in Freetown, Sierra Leone. We planned that I would accompany him and that we would stop in Monrovia, stay for a while at the Cooper Clinic and then go on to Freetown for the meeting. Our itinerary required us to fly from Nashville to New York and from New York to Monrovia. At the airport to see us off in Nashville were our son, Armah, his infant son, our grandson, Adam, and our younger daughter, Lisa. In New York, our daughter, Dawn, her husband, Nat and their two sons, Nyema and Julien, met us.

As we boarded a Pan American flight at JFK Airport in New York, little did we know that this was the last time that Miah would see our children and the only three grandchildren he would know were Nyema, Julien and Adam. All of our other grandchildren were born after he had died.

Aboard the plane, we met many interesting folks; many were going to South Africa, the final destination of that flight. One lady had the sad story that she was going to bury her mother who had died of cancer. When she found out that Miah was an oncologist, she had so many questions and I believe that, as always, he tried to be helpful.

We arrived at Roberts International Airport near Monrovia and went directly to the clinic. We planned to meet with the Cooper Clinic staff the next day, and then visit our farm in Bomi County, Liberia, before going to Freetown for the conference. Miah did meet with the clinic staff, but he never got to go to the farm. I went alone. He never got to Freetown. Miah died in his clinic on Sunday, January 29, 1984 of a heart attack.

In his comments to the Cooper Clinic staff days before his death, Miah said: "If there were one message that I came here to deliver it is that the Cooper Clinic is alive and well and will continue to be alive and well for some time to come by the Grace of God. Many who ask the question, "Could the Cooper Clinic continue?" have no need to ask that question any more because, if the Cooper Clinic can continue in the absence of Cooper, it should be obvious that it can continue."

Miah's funeral in Liberia was a grand affair. The Government of Liberia was pleased to honor him by giving him a state funeral. Many very fine tributes were paid to him and people from all walks of life traveled from near and far to pay respects. Classmates, professional and social organizations were represented. He was buried at his family's estate in Kormah, Bomi County, Liberia.

Immediately after the funeral, I returned to the U.S. to organize my affairs and return to Liberia to try to run the clinic. Our church family in Nashville, Clark Memorial United Methodist, had a memorial service for Miah. Our Meharry Medical College family with the R. F. Boyd Medical Society Auxiliary hosted a luncheon. Among the many friends who came to Nashville for the memorial service and who encouraged me after Miah's death was Mrs. Victoria Tolbert, whom I affectionately called "Mother Vic," widow of the late President William R. Tolbert. She referred to me as her "Dollbaby." Also sources of strength were Elaine and Jean Bassene, who became like my own children, and my cousin, Trypetus Padmore.

When I returned to Liberia to run the clinic, I encountered many challenges. Realizing that I could not personally continue the operation of the clinic, I remembered Miah's wish that, if ever we could not maintain the operation of the Cooper Clinic personally, he would like a religious organization to acquire it to continue to serve the people. With this in mind, I sought to sell the clinic to such an organization. The Seventh Day Adventist Church, internationally renown for its health care services, made me an offer, which I accepted. The children and I requested that the clinic be a memorial to Miah by keeping the name Cooper; and further required that no future sale of the clinic could occur without first offering it back to our family. These two points became a part of the agreement. Today, the Cooper Clinic is now the Seventh Day Adventist Cooper Memorial Hospital and continues to operate in Liberia in service to the community.

Miah would be so pleased to know how our little family has grown. Our greatest ambition always was to see that our children got the best education possible; and, fortunately, this dream is being realized. Our son, Armah Jamale Cooper, M.D. is a practicing psychiatrist at Central Regional Hospital in Butner, North Carolina. He is the former director of the R. J. Blackley Alcohol and Drug Treatment Center. He is married to Shahmeem Rajak, who has an MBA degree and teaches math. Armah has two sons, Adam Roberts Cooper and Joseph Nehemiah Cooper and two stepchildren, Jasmin and Nadeem Rajak. Our daughter, Dawn Cooper Barnes, Ph.D., is a film producer and former associate professor of Performing Arts at Howard Community College. She is co-founder of the Liberian Renaissance Foundation with her husband, Milton Nathaniel Barnes, former Liberian Ambassador to the United Nations and the United States. They are the parents of six children: Nyema, Julien, Henry, Courtney, Zwannah and Sadayah Barnes. Our daughter, Lisa Angeline Cooper, M. D., is a professor of Internal Medicine and Epidemiology at Johns Hopkins University. She is also a MacArthur Fellow. She is married to Nigel Green, a computer engineer at the Embassy of Great Britain in Washington, D.C. Lisa has one son, Donovan Cooper Patrick. Her younger son, Devin Roberts Patrick, died as an infant.

Scrapbook of Photos

College of West Africa (High School), Monrovia, Liberia.

College of West Africa Graduating Class of 1944.
Front Row: Williette Summerville, Henrietta Watkins, and Mona Twe
Middle Row: H. Nehemiah Cooper, Moses Weefur, Peter Jacob George,
Albert Kemokai, and Archibald Johnson
Back Row: Rushu Karnga, Charles McGill, Henry Cassell, Samuel Butler

H. Nehemiah Cooper, Meharry Medical School, 1954.

The Panther 1948 Yearbook, Clark College, Atlanta, GA
H. Nehemiah Cooper, Class President (right).

H. Nehemiah Cooper (center) with two Clark College professors
reviewing the chemistry mathematic textbook Cooper published, 1949.

H. Nehemiah Cooper and Izetta Roberts Cooper, 1954.

Front row: Bill and Marlene Chavis
H. Nehemiah Cooper, Izetta Roberts Cooper (back row center)
with friends, June 1955.

American gospel singer Mahalia Jackson at the Cooper home, 1970.
Front row: Agnes Dennis, Izetta Cooper, Euphemia Weeks, Willitte Jupiter.
Second row: Mary Eliza Horton, Mahalia Jackson, Ora Horton, and Corinna
Hilton Van Ee. Third Row: Rosina Grimes, three women accompanying M.
Jackson, and Lucille Brumskine.

Villa Ardalis, the Cooper home in Calpe, Spain, 1970s.

Cooper Family Home in Oldest Congotown
painted by Liberian artist J. Kollie, 1989.

H. Nehemiah Cooper with grandson Julien Barnes, 1983.

H. Nehemiah Cooper with grandson Adam Cooper, 1983.

Cooper Family in Nashville, Tennessee Christmas, 1982.
Front row: Dawn holding Adam, Mrs. Cooper holding Julien and Lisa.
Back row: Dr. Cooper, Armah (Butch), Jewell, and Nat Barnes.

Jewell Edgerton Cooper, former wife of Armah,
with their sons Joseph and Adam, 1986.

Armah (Butch) Cooper and his wife, Shahmeem, in Jamaica, 2007.

Armah (Butch) Cooper with his sons in 2006.
Adam (left) and Joseph.

The Barnes Family, 2009
Front row: Sadayah, Nat, Dawn, and Courtney
Back row: Zwannah, Nyema, Henry, and Julien

Lisa with her husband, the late George Patrick, and their sons,
Donovan Cooper Patrick and Devin Roberts Patrick (deceased), 1997.

Lisa and her husband Nigel Green with their son,
Donovan Cooper Patrick, 2007.

H. Nehemiah Cooper and Izetta Roberts Cooper, 1978
25th Wedding Anniversary Celebration

The Cooper Family
Ducor International Hotel, Monrovia, Liberia
From the left are Dawn, Mrs. Cooper, Dr. Cooper, Lisa, and Armah
25th Wedding Anniversary Celebration

The Cooper Clinic
12th Street at Gibson Avenue
Sinkor, Monrovia, Liberia

Cloth Cooper Clinic Patch

Opening Ceremony for The Cooper Clinic, March 17, 1963
Dr. H. Nehemiah Cooper speaking with Liberian
President William Tubman looking on.

Opening Ceremony for The Cooper Clinic, March 1963
From right: Angeline Cooper, R.N., Armah Cooper, Mrs. Izetta
Cooper, Mrs. Antoinette Tubman, Dr. Murrey Barclay, Secretary of
Health, Dr. H. Nehemiah Cooper, Aaron Milton, architect of the
Cooper Clinic speaking, and President W.V.S. Tubman.

Opening Day Ribbon Cutting at the Cooper Clinic, March 1963
Dr. H. Nehemiah Cooper and daughter, Dawn.

Opening Ceremony for The Cooper Clinic, March 1963
From left: Mrs. Antoinette Tubman, Rev. and Mrs. Samuel Smith.
The Smiths were H.S. teachers and mentors of Dr. Cooper.

The Cooper Clinic Staff, 1980
Izetta Roberts Cooper, front row left, and Dr. H. Nehemiah Cooper,
front row right.

Dr. H. Nehemiah Cooper with his sister, Angeline Cooper, R. N.

Opening of the Cooper Clinic Annex, 1980
Dr. H. Nehemiah Cooper and Liberia President William Tolbert, Jr.

Opening of the Cooper Clinic Annex, 1980
Lisa Cooper cuts the Opening Day ribbon as Father Edward King
looks on.

Opening of the Cooper Clinic Annex, 1980
Dr. and Mrs. Cooper accompany President and Mrs. Tolbert.

The Cooper Clinic

Dr. H. Nehemiah Cooper interviewed while attending the American Medical Association conference at Americana Hotel, July 1969.

West African College of Surgeons Postcard, Monrovia.
Dr. H. Nehemiah Cooper is on the front row, fifth from left.

West African College of Surgeons Conference, Monrovia.
Dr. H. Nehemiah Cooper is on the front row, second from left.
Dr. William R. Tolbert, Jr., President, Republic of Liberia is in white.

Dr. H. Nehemiah Cooper, President Tolbert, Matthew Walker, M.D., and delegation at the founding of the Liberian Cancer Society.

Liberian Cancer Society Founding Members
Eugenia Shaw (far left), R. Brewer, Linne Kesselly, Sofie Dunbar Cooper,
Liberia First Lady Victoria Tolbert, Emily Benjamin, Corinna Hilton Van Ee,
Liberia President William R. Tolbert, Jr., Perinne DeShield, Dr. Sobo,
Bishop Michael Francis, Dr. Avril Sherman Caesar, Dr. H. N. Cooper.

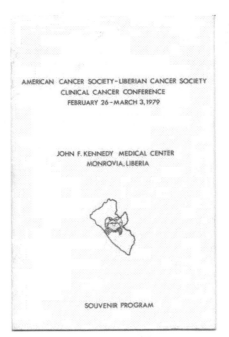

AMERICAN CANCER SOCIETY-LIBERIAN CANCER SOCIETY
CLINICAL CANCER CONFERENCE
FEBRUARY 26-MARCH 3, 1979

JOHN F. KENNEDY MEDICAL CENTER
MONROVIA, LIBERIA

SOUVENIR PROGRAM

1979 Clinical Cancer Conference Program

Dr. Cooper watches as Liberian President William R. Tolbert, Jr.,
greets LaSalle Lefall, M.D. President of the American Cancer Society
during the 1979 Clinical Cancer Conference Program.

American Cancer Society and Liberian Cancer Society
Clinical Cancer Conference Program, 1979.

Rotary International Club of Monrovia, mid-1970s.

Standing from left: Alexander Ketter, Leonard DeShield (rear), H. Nehemiah
Cooper, Clarence Parker, Bennie Warner, V.P.R.L., Joseph Richards.
Front bending from left: Joseph Togba, M.D. and Liberia President Tolbert.

Dr. H. Nehemiah Cooper, Ellen Johnson Sirleaf, and friends in
Nairobi, Kenya, 1981.

Dr. H. Nehemiah Cooper, Liberia President William R. Tolbert, Jr.,
First Lady Victoria Tolbert, and Izetta Roberts Cooper at the Coopers'
25th wedding anniversary, July 1978.

Dr. H. Nehemiah Cooper commissioned as Chief Medical Officer, John F. Kennedy Memorial Center, Monrovia, Liberia, circa 1972.

Dr. H. Nehemiah Cooper and Walter Brumskine, M.D., 1979.

Dedication of the Cobalt Teletherapy Unit, John F. Kennedy Hospital, Monrovia, Liberia, 1976. Dr. Marion Mann, Dean, Department of Radiotheraphy, Howard University School of Medicine (center standing) giving remarks. Dr. H. Nehemiah Cooper is seated to the left and President and Mrs. William Tolbert, Jr. are right of Dr. Mann.

Dr. H. Nehemiah Cooper (left), Hon. Richard Henries, Speaker, House of Representatives, Dean Mann, and President William Tolbert, Jr.

Dr. H. Nehemiah Cooper is introduced to U.S. Secretary of State
Henry Kissinger by C. Cecil Dennis, Minister of Foreign Affairs, at a
1976 dinner at the Executive Mansion in Monrovia, Liberia

Dr. H. Nehemiah Cooper and Dr. Jack Lange of Lange Medical
Publications at the Executive Mansion, Monrovia, early 1970s.

Mrs. De Lange, Lange Medical Publishers, greeting President Tolbert
as Dr. Jack Lange and Dr. H. Nehemiah Cooper look on.

Dr. and Mrs. H. Nehemiah Cooper with Fatumatta Diggs and U.S. Ambassador to Liberia W. Beverly Carter, Jr., circa 1976.

Dr. H. Nehemiah Cooper entertaining friends at Oldest Congotown residence.

Funeral services for Dr. H. Nehemiah Cooper,
First United Methodist Church, Monrovia, 1984.

First United Methodist Church on Ashmun Street, Monrovia, 1984

Armah (Butch) Cooper speaks at his father's funeral service, 1984.

Traditional dance being performed after Dr. Cooper's burial, 1984.

Henry Nehemiah Cooper, M.D.
1927 – 1984
Husband, Father, Surgeon, Humanitarian
Cooper Family Estate, Kormah, Clayashland, Liberia

A guinea fowl returning home.
Photo by Lisa Cooper Green, MD, MPH.

The Liberia Official Gazette

THE
LIBERIA OFFICIAL
GAZETTE

PUBLISHED BY AUTHORITY

VOL. 3   MONDAY, FEBRUARY 1, 1984   No. 19

EXTRAORDINARY

The Government of the Republic of Liberia announces with profound regret the death in his fifty-seventh year of:

DR. HENRY NEHEMIAH COOPER, M.D., KC, GC, KGB, KGC
FORMER CHIEF MEDICAL OFFICER,
JOHN F. KENNEDY MEMORIAL MEDICAL CENTRE
FORMER ASSOCIATE DEAN
A.M. DOGLIOTTI COLLEGE OF MEDICINE
UNIVERSITY OF LIBERIA.

This untimely event occurred on Sunday, January 29, 1984 at the Cooper Clinic in Monrovia, Liberia, at the hour of 12:30 o'clock post meridian.

Dr. Henry Nehemiah Cooper, loving husband, devoted father, reliable family man, dedicated professional, dependable friend, patriotic citizen, who deeply appreciated the hopes, desires, aspirations and longings of his fellow men, was born in the city of Monrovia, Montserrado County, Republic of Liberia on July 18, 1927, the fourth son and fourth child of the union of Mr. Charles Henry Cooper, (son of Mr. James Wesley Cooper and Mrs. Malissa Cooper) and Mrs. Maryann Dabadolo Cooper nee Johnson, (daughter of Paramount Chief Jamale Johnson and Madam Keimah Johnson).

His early years were spent at the Cooper Family Estate in Kormah, Clayashland and in Monrovia. Young Nehemiah Cooper commenced his formal education at the Mary McCritty Elementary School in Monrovia and attended High School at the College of West Africa, Monrovia, where he graduated from high school in 1944. He travelled to the United States of America in 1946 in pursuit of higher education, matriculated to Clark College, Atlanta, Georgia, graduating from that College in 1950, with the degree of Bachelor of Science, Magna Cum Laude.

That same year, he entered Meharry Medical College, Nashville, Tennessee, where he continued to demonstrate the same extraordinary scholarship that had typified his studies at Clark College. In recognition of his special talents, the faculty of Meharry Medical College presented him with a citation for outstanding scholarship in 1951. In 1952 he was admitted as a member of the Kappa Pi Medical Honor Society. In 1954 he earned the M.D. degree at Meharry, with highest honors. As a befitting capstone to an academic career which had been characterised by sustained brilliance, he

The Liberia Official Gazette

Monday, February 1, 1984, Vol 3., No. 19

EXTRAORDINARY

The Government of the Republic of Liberia announces with profound regret the death in his fifty-seventh year of:

Dr. Henry Nehemiah Cooper, M.D., KC, GC, KGB, KGC

Former Chief Medical Officer,

John F. Kennedy Memorial Medical Centre

Former Associate Dean, A.M. Dogliotti College of Medicine, University of Liberia

This untimely event occurred on Sunday, January 29, 1984 at the Cooper Clinic in Monrovia, Liberia, at the hour of 12:30 o'clock post meridian.

Dr. Henry Nehemiah Cooper, loving husband, devoted father, reliable family man, dedicated professional, dependable friend, patriotic citizen, who deeply appreciated the hopes, desires, aspirations and longings of his fellow men, was born in the city of Monrovia, Montserrado County, Republic of Liberia on July 18, 1927, the fourth son and fourth child of the union of Mr. Charles Henry Cooper, (son of Mr. James Wesley Cooper and Mrs. Melissa Cooper) and Mrs. Maryann Dabadolo Cooper need Johnson, (daughter of Paramount Chief Jamale Johnson and Madam Keimah Johnson).

His early years were spent at the Cooper Family Estate in Kormah, Clay Ashland and in Monrovia. Young Nehemiah Cooper commenced his formal education at the Mary McCritty Elementary School in Monrovia and attended High School at the College of West Africa, Monrovia, where he graduated from high school in 1944. He traveled to the United States of America in 1946 in pursuit of higher education, matriculated to Clark College, Atlanta, Georgia, graduating from that College in 1950, with the degree of Bachelor of Science, Magna Cum Laude.

That same year, he entered Meharry Medical College, Nashville, Tennessee, where he continued to demonstrate the same extraordinary scholarship that had typified his studies at Clark College. In recognition of his special talents, the faculty of Meharry Medical College presented him with a citation for outstanding scholarship in 1951. In 1952 he was admitted as a member of the Kappa Pi Medical Honor Society. In 1954 he earned the M.D. degree at Meharry, with highest honors. As a befitting capstone to an academic career which had been characterized by sustained brilliance, he was awarded the Charles Nelson Gold Medal which is awarded each year by Meharry Medical College to the Ranking Medical Graduate. Thus began a long and mutually beneficial post graduate and professional relationship with Meharry Medical College which was to continue throughout his natural life time.

Between 1954 and 1955, he undertook his internship at the Muamee Valley Hospital in Toledo, Ohio, returning to Nashville as Resident in Surgery at the George W. Hubbard Hospital, Meharry Medical College, from 1955 to 1958. From 1958 to 1959 he served as Resident Surgeon at the Memorial Sloan Kettering Center for Cancer and Allied Diseases, in New York City and again returned to Meharry Medical College in 1959, this time as Chief Resident in Surgery, which position he held until 1960 when he returned to Liberia after fifteen years of work and study in the United States of America, to make his personal contribution to national development and progress in general and to the medical profession in particular.

In recognition and appreciation of his outstanding professional preparedness and experience, the Government of Liberia was pleased to appoint him to a number of responsible professional and administrative positions in the health delivery services of the country, including: Attending Surgeon, Liberian Government Hospital, Monrovia 1961 to 1963; Chief Surgeon, Liberian Government Hospital, Monrovia 1963 to 1968; Consultant Surgeon, National Public Health Service, Monrovia, 1968 to 1972; Personal Physician to the President of Liberia, 1971; Chief Medical Officer, John F. Kennedy Medical Center, Monrovia, 1972 to 1980; Associate Dean,

A. M. Dogliotti College of Medicine, University of Liberia, 1972 to 1980; Professor of Surgery, Attending Surgeon, and Director of Tumor Clinic, John F. Kennedy Medical Center, 1973.

As Chief Medical Officer of the John F. Kennedy Medical Center, Monrovia, Professor of Surgery and Associate Dean of the A. M. Dogliotti College of Medicine, University of Liberia, he formulated and fought for the implementation of a number of policies and programs which have had a fundamental and lasting impact on the entire Health Care Delivery System of Liberia. Outstanding among his accomplishments in this area was a Unified Outreach Program, with the Medical School as a central axis, and with the Ministry of Health and the Medical Center in cooperation. To this end he was instrumental in the planning and supervision of staff development as well as in the formation of the functional medical center from four hospitals in the Monrovia area, with a total bed capacity of 750 and with medical personnel, including house staff, of 150 physicians.

Another of his major accomplishments was the organization of the undergraduate medical teaching program at the A. M. Dogliotti College of Medicine in 1972, which later evolved and developed into a post-graduate program by 1976. This institution now produces each year a procession of well qualified physicians and other medical personnel who hail from all parts of Liberia and from foreign countries, both near and far.

Perhaps the most sterling achievement of Dr. H. Nehemiah Cooper, and the most concrete manifestation of his contribution to the growth and development of the medical profession in Liberia, was the founding in 1962 and the subsequent development of the Cooper Clinic for Diagnosis and Special Surgery, located on 12th Street in Sinkor, Monrovia. The Cooper Clinic was founded as a private poly/clinic which now has a 30-bed in patient capacity, staffed by six physicians. The clinic continues to function as a referral unit for several hospitals in the interior of Liberia, and has become proficient in handling medical evacuation escort services on a worldwide basis. Throughout the years since its founding, it has consistently maintained exceptionally high standards of medical practice, and remains today one of the finest examples of its kind anywhere in the world.

Dr. Cooper was also actively involved in the regional organization of medical education in Africa, being a Founding Fellow of the West African College of Surgeons. He served that organization as an Executive Council Member and Vice President from 1975 to 1977. He also participated in the negotiations that led to the formation of the West African Post-Graduate Medical College and the West African Health Secretariat.

Dr. Cooper represented the Republic of Liberia at several sessions of the World Health Assembly in Geneva and was Principal Advisor to the Government of Liberia on health policy. He also served on a number of delegations to several international conferences, including the United Nations General Assembly.

A man of International repute, he was well respected by his professional colleagues in many countries. He was a member of many professional associates, including the Liberian Medical and Dental Association of which he was a past President. In recognition of his sterling qualities and his unstinting dedication to and absolute involvement with the enhancement and development of the medical profession, his colleagues in Liberia saw fit to honor him with the Distinguished Service Award of the Liberian Medical and Dental Association in 1973. Other professional associations of which Dr. Cooper was a member or fellow include:

- The American Medical Association – Special Honorary Member, 1969

- The National Medical Association (USA) – Member

- The West African College of Surgeons – Founding Fellow

- The International College of Surgeons – Fellow, 1962

- The American College of Surgeons – Fellow, 1964

- The American Cancer Society – Member

- The Society of Surgical Oncology – Member

- The Societé International de Chirurgie – Member

- The American Public Health Association – Member

Dr. Henry Nehemiah Cooper was also active in social and civic activities. HE was an innovator and a natural leader. He founded the Liberian Cancer Society and served that organization as an Executive Board Member and Chairman of its Professional Education Committee. He was a Member and Past-President of the Rotary Club of Monrovia and a Member of the Board of Trustees of the YMCA. A devout Christian and Churchman, he was a Member of the Congregation of the First United Methodist Church of Monrovia, and served as a Member of its Administrative Board.

He belonged to a number of fraternities, including Omega Psi Phi, Beta Theta Boule, and Sigma Pi Phi. He was admitted to the Alpha Kappa Mu National Honor Society in 1948, and the Alpha Omega Alpha Honor Medical Society in 1979.

He received the following decorations from The Liberian Government for outstanding service to the Government and people of Liberia:

- Commander, Order of the Star of Africa – 1964
- Grand Commander, Humane Order of African Redemption – 1968
- Knight Great Band, Humane Order of African Redemption – 1975
- Knight Grand Commander of the Most Venerable Order of the Pioneers – 1978

He also received decorations from the Government of the Republic of Gambia, the Federal Republic of Germany, the Republic of Haiti, the Kingdom of Greece, and the Kingdom of Saudi Arabia.

His business affiliations included: President and Chairman of the Board, H. N. Cooper Enterprises, Inc. and member of the Board of Directors of five other companies.

On the occasion of his resignation as Chief Medical Officer of the John F. Kennedy Medical Center, effective December 31, 1979, he penned his "Valedictory Thoughts" to the medical staff of the Center on November 1, 1979, exactly two months before the effective date of his resignation, in words which are worthy of remembering. Excepts from his "Valedictory Thoughts" follow:

"My remarks on parting must be in at least two parts. The first part must acknowledge the chaotic, undermanned and under-funded organization that had to be shaped into a viable Medical Staff to lead the thrust into a new era of Health Care Delivery. Our original idea of a unified outreach program, together with a central axis of the Medical School, with the Ministry of Health and the Medical Center in cooperation, remains the basis of today's operations. It was considered radical in 1972... Our real accomplishment may actually have been in the partial eradication of the overwhelming inferiority complex that our people seem to have about their doctors and their health care. Only time will tell.

"Whatever my accomplishments may have been, they are punctuated by the number of incomplete projects I am leaving; some very near completion, others more distant. All of them, I believe, are worthy of completion...

They include the following:

1. The Learning Resources Studio
2. The House Staff Apartments
3. The JFK Medical Center Staff Recreation Association
4. Medical Staff Housing to support the Exchange Program
5. (The Prosthetic Workshop has barely escaped the category of incomplete projects)....

"The second dimension of my remarks is more profound. It has little to do with buildings, gadgets and budgets. It is largely intangible. It must acknowledge the great personal sacrifices made by many of you in leaving the allure and professional satisfaction of working in some of the most advanced institutions in the world, and coming home to improvise and modify – frequently without the understanding or sympathy of your countrymen...

"But as noble as these sacrifices may be, they are not more than our duty; and they are punctuated by a need that I consider to be most urgent... There is a need for Professional discipline that far surpasses any need we have today. Yes, even including equipment and money!...

"If we increase our militancy in the guarding of professional discipline, absolute dedication to our patients comes naturally and without strain. While militancy in the safeguarding of "perks" and pay is a legal right, it must be forever secondary to our professional obligations...

"There is a bright future ahead. We can either tarnish it or amplify its glitter. The choice for fortunately is within our control. I leave you with PEACE, but I hope it will be a restless peace that is ever more demanding in the quest for excellence!"

Dr. Henry Nehemiah Cooper was married on July 11, 1953 to Izetta Roberts Cooper, who survives him. This happy union was blessed with three children, Armah Jamale Cooper, M.D., Izetta Dawn Cooper Barnes, and Lisa Angeline Catherine Cooper.

He leaves to mourn his loss his wife and three children, a son-in-law, Mr. Milton Nathaniel Barnes; a daughter-in-law, Mrs. Jewel Egerton Cooper; three grand children, Nyema Barnes, Julien Nathaniel Barnes and Adam Roberts Egerton Cooper; two brothers, Samuel David Cooper and Charles Ernest Cooper; four sisters, Angeline S. Cooper, Maryann Cooper Melton, Marion Amanda Cooper Givens and Rosalind Cooper Richards; one foster brother, Francis D. Cooper and a host of aunts, uncles, nephews, cousins, grand nieces, grand nephews, and many other relatives and friends.

On Saturday, February 4, 1984, at four o'clock post meridian, the mortal remains of the late Dr. Henry Nehemiah Cooper will be removed from the Grace Brownell Funeral Parlours and taken to the Cooper Clinic on 12 Street in Sinkor, Monrovia. At five-thirty o'clock post meridian on Saturday the body will be taken from the Cooper Clinic at the First United Methodist Church on Ashmun Street, Monrovia, where wake will be kept form nine-o'clock post meridian until midnight. Funeral services will be held to the First United Methodist Church, Ashmun Street on Sunday, February 5, 1984, at two o'clock post meridian. Thereafter, the funeral cortege will proceed to the Cooper Family Estate, Kormah, Clayashland, where interment will take place.

As a mark of last respect to the late Dr. Henry Nehemiah Cooper, M.D., KC, GC, KGB, KGC, Former Chief Medical Officer, John F. Kennedy Memorial Medical Center, Former Associate Dean, A. M. Dogliotti College of Medicine, University of Liberia, it is herby ordered and directed that on the day of interment the flag of the Republic be flown at half-staff from all public buildings in the City of Monrovia, Montserrado County, from eight o'clock ante meridian to six o'clock post meridian.

BY ORDER OF THE HEAD OF STATE

Ernest Eastman
Minister of Foreign Affairs

Ministry of Foreign Affairs
Monrovia, Liberia
February 3, 1984

Tributes to the Late H. Nehemiah Cooper, M.D.

A man of rare intellect

A man of great compassion

His death has created a void not only in your life, but the lives of colleagues at Meharry Medical College and the lives of people worldwide.

- Axel Hansen, M.D. FACS
(Dr. Cooper's teacher at Meharry Medical College)

A former President of the Liberian Medical and Dental Association, a friend, a colleague and one of the finest examples of a true physician. He was never intimidated by new ideas and thrived on challenges…a stimulating teacher of doctors… his life was the story of a man in quest of excellence. He leaves a legacy that will challenge and inspire generations of Liberian doctors in years to come. He has built for himself a monument greater that any of us can ever erect to him… He lives in our hearts….He belongs to the ages….

- Wilfred Sei Boayue, M.D. MPH, FACS,
President Liberian Medical and Dental Association

Dr. Cooper's career as a health care professional was indeed one of enviable distinction and we will miss his contributions in the Department of Surgery as well as his leadership as Director of the International Center for Health Services…

- David Satcher, M.D. Ph.D.
President, Meharry Medical College
(In a letter to Dr. & Mrs. Philip Nicholas thanking them for attending the funeral and reading the resolutions from Meharry Medical College.)

His name – Henry Nehemiah Cooper – a household name...It has been said you give but little when you give your possessions. It is when you give yourself that you truly give. He gave his knowledge, his skills and untiringly of himself to the community, to his colleagues, to students, both graduates and post graduate...for contributions in widening the scope of post-graduate training of the college...designer of the symbol on the college ...a legend in his lifetime... If posterity were to ask the Muse of Time to name the Greats in the Medical profession in West Africa, she would dip her pen in the golden sunlight and write across the blue sky, 'Henry Nehemiah Cooper, M.D.'...During his term as Chief Medical Officer of the John F. Kennedy Medical Center, the Post Graduate Medical Education Program was initiated and implemented. He did not restrict himself to administrative responsibility, his impressive desire to provide service to the sick led him to establish a Tumor Clinic in Surgical Encology and the establishment of the second Radio Therapy Unit on the West African Coast... This idea overflowed into the community and he became a motivating force behind the establishment of the Liberian Cancer Society... Mourning his passing away today can be seen from the strata of society because he firmly believed in the dignity of the individual.

- The West African Post Graduate Medical College,
  The West African College of Surgeons

A dear friend, fellow physician, brother, teacher. He worked hard at times under difficulties to help his countrymen particularly the less fortunate. He contributed greatly to medical care in his homeland and inspired colleagues in neighboring countries and internationally. A wonderful husband, a loving and patient father and for all a kindly healer and great humanitarian.

- Delores and Jack Lang
  Lang Medical Publications

A founding member of the Association of Surgeons of West Africa, now the West African College of Surgeons...showed his love for peoples of West Africa by his constant concern for their welfare through a standard of Surgical Practice. He taught by example. We salute the memory of Dr Cooper, a distinguished surgeon, philanthropist, humanitarian, west African... We salute his contributions to the growth of surgical science in Africa, to the art of surgery around the world and to the welfare of his fellowman...the college will record its tribute in the permanency of Nehemiah's contributions to growth and development...On behalf of the President, Council, Fellows...

- Professor T. F. Solanke, Past President of the College & Dr. Adewunmi, Assistant Secretary General for Professor A.A. Adebonjo FWACS, Secretary General

The Board of Regents of the American College of Surgeons has learned with deep regrets of the death of Henry N. Cooper, M.D...To his bereaved family and friends we tender sympathy and as a mark of our respect to his memory , we desire to transmit to them this memorial...In witness whereof we have caused the common seal of the American College of Surgeons to be herewith affixed

- The President, Chairman of the Board of Regents & Directors of the American College of Surgeons

Founder- the Liberian Cancer Society with a group of medical and non-medical individuals in 1977....In 1979 the Liberian Cancer Society became a member of the International Cancer Society. Dr. Cooper was a great leader, whose desire to help cancer patients led him to establish a Tumor Clinic at the John F. Kennedy Medical Center. Through his initiative friends at Howard University, Washington, D.C. U.S.A. donated a Cobalt Unit for the treatment of cancer, free of charge to Liberians as well non-Liberians of neighboring countries...

- The Liberian Cancer Society

The measure of a man is not only what people believe about him, but also what good things he has achieved for himself, his family and his fellow man...Dr. Cooper was such a man ..The high standard he set and accomplished for his clinic, his selfless service and dedication to his profession, the respect and love of his colleagues, his concern for his staff and employees whether it was personal or professional, testify to this. The founder of Cooper Clinic, our boss, whom we nicknamed, 'Joe Blow', was a wonderful all around person. We loved him...the highest tribute we can pay Dr. Cooper is to maintain the high standards expected of us – to maintain the service to humanity and to be a source of love and consolation to those who are in need...

- The Cooper Clinic Staff

Meharry, in general, and the International Center for Health Service...has experienced a great loss because of Dr. Cooper's death. Even tough he was our boss,, the working relationship was like that of a colleague, a friend, brother and advisor. He brought to the Center a rich medical as well as a high administrative experience on the international level, being familiar with the African Health Care Delivery System. The impact of his teaching and advice will help us to face the challenges of the future...Dr. Cooper's family is well known to the center. We worked with Lisa as a participant in one of our summer programs even before her father came to the Center, became acquainted with Armah, who was a medical student and also got to know through French classes. Mrs. Cooper has taken part, as well, supporting our programs both here and abroad. Thank you and May God bless you.

- The Staff
  International Center for Health Services
  Meharry Medical Center

Dr. H. Nehemiah Cooper was Chief Medical Officer of the JFKMC from 1972 -1980. During his tenure, the Center grew from three small almost separate health service facilities to a modern medical center with four hospitals and the TNIMA that has more than seven vocational schools. He supervised staffing and staff development, the formation and organization of both the undergraduate and post-graduate medical training program, the in-service training of general duty medical officer corps and cohesive interdisciplinary diagnostic and therapeutic health services thus actually converting the JFKMC into a functional modern medical center serving as a referral hospital, a training institution and specialized resource reservoir.

He more than any other single individual mapped out the course and direction of this institution making it what it is today...No one can, therefore, really innumerate the accomplishments of this man, nor anticipate the dreams he had or would have had as far as they relate to the development of the JFKMC and the National Health Care Delivery System of Liberia in general. Two things, however, must be stated here: 1) the appointment of Dr. H. Nehemiah Cooper as Chief Medical Officer of the JFKMC in 1972 was the single most important decision that has ever been made affecting that institution, 2) he was a leader, a clinician and an intellectual scholar who commanded the respect of everyone most especially his peers....It will be difficult to replace him...

Paraphrasing the words of Marcus Antonius, we can say only: 'Here was a Man, when comes such another?' ... In his death we are witnessing the passing of an era – a period of truly great clinicians and medical doctors of our times. The species of men to which he belonged is dying out and like the great dinosaurs will become immortalized only in the fossil remains of their deeds and accomplishments. So as we pay our final respects to this man, we are actually engraving these words on his gravestone: 'Dr. H. Nehemiah Cooper 1927-1984, In those days there were giants who walked upon earth; we cannot honor you, Chief, for through your life of scholarship, service and dedication you have indeed honored yourself more than we ever hope to do. In parting we can by say, 'Farewell, Chief, farewell Teacher, farewell, Friend. May the Eternal Rest that you have earned be yours!'"

- V. Kanda Golokai, M.D.,
  Chief Medical Officer FWACS
  The Medical Staff JFKMC

This work [the <u>Cancer Registration in Africa with Particular Reference to Liberia: 1973-1980</u>] is dedicated to Mrs. C Hilton van Ee, the first President of the Liberian Cancer Society and to the memory of the late Dr. Henry Nehemiah Cooper, M.D. former Chief Medical Officer of the John F. Kennedy Memorial Centre, Monrovia, Liberia.

- A.O. Sobo, M.D.

Dr. Henry Nehemiah Cooper was a remarkable human being, who throughout his adult lifetime was a surgical scholar and educated man in the truest sense, a dedicated servant to his nation and his medical alma mater, Meharry, and always a gentleman. He served not only the community in his native Liberia, but internationally. He continued his contributions to Meharry, serving as host and preceptor to Meharry Medical residents at the John F. Kennedy Medical Center, Monrovia, Liberia while Chief Medical Officer of that institution, and at the same time clinical professor in Meharry's Department of Surgery. In 1981 he joined the full time faculty as Professor of Surgery. His contributions to society are many and detailed elsewhere. To us, his colleagues, he was a distinguished surgeon, a superb teacher, a delightful friend and a man who cared dearly.

- The Department of Surgery
  Meharry Medical College

I knew him as our father, as my best friend and my confidante. He was very supportive of his children and we had a rapport with him that transcended emotional and psychological spheres. He adored our mother. My father was a great humanitarian. He often spoke of his philosophy of life, "There are so many people who helped me along the way, I only feel it fair that I help others along the way." Many can testify to his helpful services.

- Armah J. Cooper, M.D.
  (Dr. Cooper's son)

Memorial and Scholarship Funds

The Henry Nehemiah Cooper Post Graduate Reading Room of the John F. Kennedy Hospital, Monrovia Liberia was established September 18, 1986 in memory of Dr. H.N. Cooper, first Chief Medical Officer of the medical center

The Seventh Day Adventist Cooper Memorial Hospital established January 1986 in Monrovia, Liberia, formerly the Cooper Clinic, continues to memorialize its founder, Dr. H.N. Cooper. It was Dr. Cooper's wish that if ever the Cooper Clinic could not be maintained as a private family-owned medical facility, it would be turned over to a religious institution and continue to serve the sick.

The Henry Nehemiah Cooper, M.D. Memorial Award at Meharry Medical College in Nashville, Tennessee, was established in 1984 by the family and friends of the late Dr. Cooper who was Professor of Surgery, Founder/Director of the Cooper Clinic, Monrovia Liberia, as a living memorial to him. The award presentation is in the form of a cash prize representing the accrued interest on the principal fund. It is presented to an outstanding and needy medical student in the Department of Surgery.

Donations to this fund may be made to Meharry Medical College – Henry Nehemiah Cooper, M.D. Scholarship Fund and mailed to:

> Henry Nehemiah Cooper, M.D. Scholarship Fund
> Meharry Medical College
> School of Medicine
> Office of Student/Academic Affairs
> 1005 Dr. D.B. Todd, Jr. Blvd.
> Nashville, TN 37208-3599

Bibliography By and About Dr. Cooper

The following are articles, textbooks, and speeches by Henry Nehemiah Cooper, M.D.

Cooper, H.N. "Address on the Occasion of the 74th Anniversary of the Rotary Club of Monrovia," Liberia, February 23, 1979.

_____. Annual Report of the Chief Medical Officer of John F. Kennedy Medical Center, Monrovia, November 2, 1973.

_____. "Background Paper on the Proposed Health Care Plan JFK Medical Center," October 1971.

_____. Chemical Arithmetic for Beginners. Clark College, Atlanta, Georgia, October 1949.

_____. "Cholera." Speech delivered on the Occasion of the Opening of the Inter-regional Training Course on Cholera Control, Monrovia, Liberia, January 10, 1974.

_____. "Choriocarcinoma – Presenting as a Solitary Pulmonary Metastasis" presentation to the Tumor Clinic, John F. Kennedy Medical Center, Monrovia, 1977.

_____. "Chronic Liver Disease; Elusive Illness" on NOVA, produced by Public Television Stations by grants from TRW, Inc. and National Science Foundation. WGBH Educational Foundation, Boston, Massachusetts, 1980.

_____. "Foresight Prevents Blindness." Speech delivered on the Occasion of the Celebration of World Health Day, Monrovia, Liberia, April 7, 1976.

_____. "Health Crises in Africa." Presentation to the Second Annual Conference of the Association of African Physicians in North Africa, Inc. Washington, D.C., May 20, 1983.

_____. "The Interdependence of Government and Mission Facilities in Delivery of Health Care." Presented at the First African Conference of Christian Medicine, Monrovia, Liberia, January 21-24, 1974.

_____. Introductory Statement on the Occasion of the Dedication of the Cobalt Teletherapy Unit of the John F. Kennedy Medical Center, Monrovia, Liberia, May 11, 1976.

_____. "Management of Far-Advanced Mammary Carcinoma" JFK Series 1: 1973-1976.

_____. "Memorandum to the Board of Directors Reorganization of the Medical Staff and Services of the J.F. Kennedy Medical Center, Monrovia, Liberia," a five year plan for staff development. March 14, 1972.

_____. "The New Technology: Implications for Surgical Practice in Developing Countries." Read by Walter Brumskine, M.D. at the 24th Annual Conference of the West African College of Surgeons, Freetown, Sierra Leone, January 23-28, 1984.

_____. "Of Time and the Art." Speech to the Conference of Peace Corps Medical Officers at the Ducor Intercontinental Hotel, Monrovia, Liberia, October 3, 1979.

_____. "On the Tenth Anniversary of the Founding of the Liberian Medical Association," Address. Monrovia, Liberia, November 24, 1974.

_____. Presented paper to the West African Consultative Association. Monrovia, Liberia, October 24, 1978.

_____. "Report of the Chief Medical Officer John F. Kennedy Memorial National Medical Center: a Summary of Status and a Look Forward Towards the New Decade," Monrovia, Liberia, July 1979.

_____. Report to the Government of the Republic of Liberia on the First Seminar on Education in Africa Held at Yaounde, Cameroon, March 22-29, 1966.

_____. "A Review of Experience with Diagnostic Urography in the Cooper Clinic, Monrovia, Liberia, January 1968 – June 16, 1969.

_____. Speech delivered to the G.W. Gibson High School Red Cross Association. Monrovia, Liberia, June 15, 1979.

_____. "Surgery of the Biliary Tract: Recent Experiences at the John F. Kennedy Memorial Hospital: Journal of the Liberian Medical Association, April 1974: 18-20.

_____. "Towards the Seventies: A Mandate for Change by Henry Nehemiah Cooper, Class of 1944," College of West Africa Alumni Review, Vol. 1 No. 1, March 1972.

_____. "Tumors of the Head and Neck: Problems & Diagnosis Management in West Africa," JFK Series, Liberian Medical and Dental Association Journal, 1974.

_____. "Tumors of the Head and Neck in Liberia," JFK Series. West African College of Surgeons Journal, 1977.

_____. " Vahun, a Medical Profile of an Isolated Liberian Village, Monrovia, Liberia, August 1974.

_____. "Valedictory Thoughts – Memorandum to the Medical Staff of John F. Kennedy Medical Center, Monrovia, Liberia," November 1, 1979.

_____ and Robert S. Schlinder, M.D.(Surgeon, ELWA Hospital, Paynesville, Liberia), "A Clinical Symposium on Surgical Diseases of the Ano-Rectal Region." Presented at the Ninth Scientific Session of the Liberian Medical Association, September 30, 1965.

The following are references to publications that mention Dr. Henry N. Cooper:

Adebonojo, Professor S.A. Secretary-General. "Mrs. Cooper & Family, Monrovia, Liberia." West African College of Surgeons. College Ouest Africain des Chirugiens, February 6, 1984.

"The American Negro in College 1953 – 1954." The Crisis, Aug/Sept 1954. See page 407 for text and page 410 for photo of Dr. Cooper.

"Clark Graduate Opens Clinic" Atlanta Daily World, Atlanta, Georgia, Sunday June 23, 1963

"The Cooper Clinic Hospital, Diagnostic Laboratories and Health Club. 12th Street and Gibson Avenue, Sinkor, Monrovia, Liberia," a brochure, 1962.

"Cooper Hopes to Expand Meharry's International Care Center." United Methodist Reporter, Clark Clarion Edition, Clark Memorial United Methodist Church, Nashville, TN, vol. 128, no. 43, April 2, 1982. p1.

Cooper, Izetta Roberts, and Kyra E. Hicks. Liberia: A Visit Through Books. Lulu.com, 2008.

"Dancing and YMCA Contributions." The Ducor Society Bulletin (Monrovia, Liberia), vol. 1, no. 8, March 4, 1966, p.1. Dr. and Mrs. Cooper are photographed dancing.

Daramola, Professor Taiwo. "Feasibility Study of A. M. Dogliotti College of Medicine. University of Liberia." August 1-21, 1994.

"Doctors' Group Apologizes to Black Physicians for Racism." St. Louis Post-Dispatch. Nation. Friday, July 11, 2008: 1, 14. American Medical Association issues a formal apology for more than a century of policies it now regrets.

"Dr. Henry Nehemiah Cooper." The Liberian Official Gazette Extraordinary. Government of the Republic of Liberia, Monrovia, vol. 3, no. 19, February 1, 1984.

Dunn, D. Elwood, Carl Patrick Burrowes, and Amos J. Beyan. Historical Dictionary of Liberia. Lanham, MD: Scarecrow, 2001. See pp. 88 – 89 for entry on Dr. Cooper.

"First Private All Liberian Clinic for Special Surgery Dedicated. Dr. Tubman Performs Ceremony." The Listener Daily. Monrovia, Liberia, vol. 13, no. 297, March 1963.

Goldsmith, Robert and Donald Heyneman, editors. Tropical Medicine and Parasitology. Norwalk, CN: Appleton & Lange, 1989. Chapter on Surgery in the Tropics. Outline and Manuscript submitted May 15, 1983 and June 23, 1983 by Henry N. Cooper, M.D. Letter of November 23, 1983 from Robert Goldsmith, M.D. and Donald Heyneman, Ph.D. primary editors, "Thank you for your contributions... your creative efforts are responsible for the book. We are confident you will be pleased with what you have wrought."

"H. N. Cooper, M.D. Dies in Liberia." Meharry Alumni Newsletter. Spring 1984, vol. 6, no. 3. p. 5.

Harris, Joseph E., editor. Global Dimensions of the African Diaspora. Washington, D.C.: Howard University Press, 1993. The chapter "Howard and Meharry: Training African Physicians" includes mention of Dr. Cooper on p. 118.

Horton, A. Romeo. For Country, Africa, and My People. Accra: Ghana Universities Press, 2005. See page 216 for Dr. Cooper and page 304 for the Cooper Clinic founding.

Leffall, LaSalle D. Jr. No Boundaries: A Cancer Surgeon's Odyssey. Washington, DC: Howard University Press, 2005. See page 128.

Macamo, Elisio Salvado. Negotiating Modernity: Africa's Ambivalent Experience. Dakar: Codesia Books [u.a.], 2005. page 46.

"Medical Library Established at J.F.K." Sunday Observer. Monrovia, Liberia, vol. 3, no. 4, September 28, 1986, p1.

Meharry Medical College, Department of Pastoral Services. "Resolution – Henry N. Cooper, M.D." A copy of the resolution, to be retained by the Archives of Meharry Medical College, was signed by John G. Corry, D.Min., Director Pastoral Ministry and David Satcher, M.D., President, January 31, 1984.

Patterson, K. David. "Disease and Medicine in African History: A Bibliographical Essay." History in Africa Journal, pp.141-148.

Patton, Adell Jr. "Dr. Henry Nehemiah Cooper, M.D." In Emmanuel Akyeampong and Henry Louis Gates, Jr., Editors in Chief, and Steven J. Nivens, Executive Editor. Dictionary of African Biography. New York: Oxford University Press, 2011.

Patton, Adell Jr. Physicians, Colonial Racism and Diaspora in West Africa. Gainesville, Florida: The University Press of Florida, 1996.

Tolbert, William R. Presidential Papers: Documents, Diary, and Record of Activities of the Chief Executive. Monrovia, Republic of Liberia: Press Division of the Executive Mansion, 1976. See pages 262, 278.

About the Co-Authors

Dawn Cooper Barnes, Ph.D. and Mrs. Izetta R. Cooper

Izetta R. Cooper is a retired librarian and lives in Columbia, Maryland. She is the author of *Liberia: A Visit Through* Books (2008).

Dawn Cooper Barnes, Ph.D. is a filmmaker, dancer, choreographer, college professor and producer of the documentary films *Cry of the Pepperbird: A Story of Liberia* and *The Spiritual Nature of African Dance: The Traditional Dances of Liberia.*

Kyra E. Hicks is a market professional and author of the children's book *Martha Ann's Quilt for Queen Victoria.*

Liberia – A Visit Through Books
A Selected Annotated Bibliography &
Reflections of a Liberian Librarian
ISBN: 978-0-557-02053-9

Izetta R. Cooper has loved books since she was a child. *Liberia – A Visit Through Books* is part biography and part bibliography. Within its covers, you will learn about the woman who:
- Lovingly raised three children and several foster children while supporting her husband's medical career
- Introduced the Dewey Decimal System to the University of Liberia Library
- Served as Library Consultant for the Presidential Library of the Executive Mansion for President William V. S. Tubman
- Hosted the ELTV television show, The World of Books
- Compiled a bibliography of more than 230 historical books on Liberia.

The Spiritual Nature of African Dance:
The Traditional Dances of Liberia
Aurora Productions, Monrovia, Liberia, 2002.
Written, directed and narrated by Dawn Cooper Barnes, Ph.D.

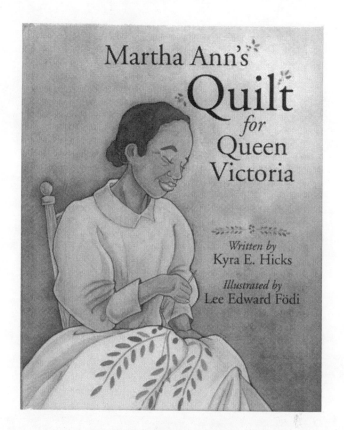

Martha Ann's Quilt for Queen Victoria
ISBN: 1-933285-59-1

Martha Ann is twelve years old when Papa finally purchases her freedom from slavery and moves the family from Tennessee to Liberia. On Market Days, Martha Ann watches the British navy patrolling the Liberian coast to stop slave catchers from kidnapping family and neighbors and forcing them back into slavery.

Martha Ann decides to thank Queen Victoria in person for sending the navy. But first, she has to save money for the 3,500–mile voyage, find a suitable gift for the queen, and withstand the ridicule of those who learn of her impossible dream to meet the Queen of England.

Kyra E. Hicks presents the true story of Martha Ann Ricks (1817–1910), a sister–in–law of Moses Ricks, a benefactor of the famed Liberian Ricks Institute.

Made in the USA
Lexington, KY
28 June 2011